RESOURCE
BOOKS FOR
TEACHERS
series editor
ALAN MALEY

GAMES FOR CHILDREN

Gordon Lewis with Günther Bedson

OXFORD
UNIVERSITY PRESS

Oxford University Press
Great Clarendon Street, Oxford OX2 6DP

Oxford New York
Auckland Bangkok Buenos Aires Cape Town
Chennai Dar es Salaam Delhi Hong Kong
Istanbul Karachi Kolkata Kuala Lumpur
Madrid Melbourne Mexico City Mumbai
Nairobi São Paulo Shanghai Singapore
Taipei Tokyo Toronto

with an associated company in Berlin

Oxford and *Oxford English*
are trade marks of Oxford University Press

ISBN 0 19 437224 3

© Oxford University Press 1999

First published 1999
Fourth impression 2002

Illustrations by David Eaton

Cover illustration by Andrew Wright
© Oxford University Press

Typeset by Oxford University Press

Printed in China

Acknowledgements

First and foremost I would like to thank Katja Prößdorf-Lewis for her tireless efforts in reviewing the manuscript. In addition, a great thank-you goes out to all the teachers at Lewis Languages in Berlin, Frankfurt, Heidelberg, and Cologne who contributed ideas and tested the games in their classes. In particular I would like to mention Lauri Smith, Laura Shaffer, Claire Coles, Gretchen Iverson, Martha Parsey, and Dee Leckie: all great and creative teachers. Many of their ideas were the sparks which triggered off finished games.

Finally, I would like to thank Julia Sallabank for leading us successfully through the editing process and helping us broaden our focus from Germany to a whole world of children.

This book is dedicated to Nicholas and Kira-Sophie Lewis

Contents

The authors and series editor

Gordon Lewis studied languages and linguistics at Georgetown University, Washington D.C. (B.S.) and at the Monterey Institute of International Studies, Monterey, California (M.S.). He began teaching English in Vienna, Austria, where he taught numerous private clients of all ages and worked in the company service of Inlingua as well. In 1988 he moved to Berlin, where he continued to teach privately. In December 1989, together with an East German partner, he founded Atlantic Connections, the first private language school in the GDR. Today the Children's Language School has branches in Berlin, Frankfurt am Main, Heidelberg, and Cologne. Gordon Lewis currently lives in Munich, where he concentrates on teacher training and curriculum development. He also taught in Russia and was a member of the EC Commission Team of Experts visiting Moscow State University, where he was responsible for evaluating the Philological Faculties and the Faculty of Modern Languages for the TACIS Program.

Günther Bedson is the director for the North-East region of Germany of the Children's Language School. He also conducts teacher training seminars with Gordon Lewis throughout Germany. Günther Bedson is from Wolverhampton, England, but studied English at the Free University of Berlin, where he was awarded a German teaching degree. He has been with Lewis Languages since 1993.

Alan Maley worked for The British Council from 1962 to 1988, serving as English Language Officer in Yugoslavia, Ghana, Italy, France, and China, and as Regional Representative in South India (Madras). From 1988 to 1993 he was Director-General of the Bell Educational Trust, Cambridge. From 1993 to 1998 he was Senior Fellow in the Department of English Language and Literature of the National University of Singapore. He is currently a freelance consultant and Director of the graduate English programme at Assumption University, Bangkok. Among his publications are *Literature*, in this series, *Beyond Words*, *Sounds Interesting*, *Sounds Intriguing*, *Words*, *Variations on a Theme*, and *Drama Techniques in Language Learning* (all with Alan Duff), *The Mind's Eye* (with Françoise Grellet and Alan Duff), *Learning to Listen* and *Poem into Poem* (with Sandra Moulding), and *Short and Sweet*. He is also Series Editor for the Oxford Supplementary Skills series.

Foreword

The pedagogical value of games in language learning at all levels has been well documented. Apart from their motivational value as an enjoyable form of activity, they provide a context in which the language is embedded. This context is 'authentic' in the sense that the game creates its own world: for the duration of the game, it replaces external reality. Games also create the circumstances for meaningful repetition. Furthermore, the 'same' game can be played many times yet never produce identical outcomes. Needless to say, games also ensure that the players interact with each other, and this interaction is usually played out in language.

For younger learners games have even greater appeal. Children are curiously paradoxical. They can be both committed to co-operation and, at the same time, fiercely competitive. They love the security of routine and the predictability of rules, yet they are often amazingly unpredictable and creative. They love to have fun, yet they dedicate themselves with deadly seriousness to the activities they engage in. It is not surprising therefore that games are so popular with children; games too involve both co-operation and competition, rules and unpredictability, enjoyment and serious commitment.

This new book of games for younger learners amply demonstrates these qualities. The authors have put together a rich and varied selection of games for children. Many of them have been devised by the authors and are therefore completely original. Some well-tried favourites have also been included, often with a new twist. All the games described here have been thoroughly tested with real learners. This collection is likely to prove to be the authoritative text on games for young learners for some years to come.

Alan Maley

Introduction

Who is this book for?

This book is for all teachers of English as a Foreign Language working with young children between the ages of four and twelve. It can be used by pre-school and primary school teachers as an extension of the general school curriculum as well as by parents in an informal private atmosphere. The games presented can stand alone or be used to complement an existing coursebook or syllabus.

Why use games in the EFL classroom?

Games are fun and children like to play them. That in itself is a strong argument for incorporating them in the EFL classroom. Playing games is a vital and natural part of growing up and learning. Through games children experiment, discover, and interact with their environment. Not to include games in the classroom would be to withhold from the children an essential tool for understanding their world; a world which the language teacher seeks to enlarge through the experience of a foreign language.

Games add variation to a lesson and increase motivation by providing a plausible incentive to use the target language. Remember that for many children between four and twelve years, especially the youngest, language learning will not be the key motivational factor. Games can provide this stimulus. The game context makes the foreign language immediately useful to the children. It brings the target language to life. The game makes the reasons for speaking plausible even to reluctant children.

What is a language game?

What distinguishes a language game from other communicative activities in the primary EFL classroom? Certainly, language games are fun. But all activities in a primary classroom should be. Games are also task based: English is a tool for the children to reach a goal which is not directly language related. Craft activities in the target language are also an example of this, as are songs. But that doesn't make them games. A stricter definition is necessary for the purpose of a language games book.

What differentiates language games from other activities in the EFL classroom is the presence of a visible set of rules which guide the children's actions, and an element of strategy—children must successfully apply their language (and other) skills. Games can be competitive, but this is not a precondition. Children can also employ their language skills strategically in co-operative games, where a group works together to achieve certain goals.

Language games are a healthy challenge to a child's analytical thought. The rules of the game set clear limits within which the children's natural decision-making processes must function. With beginners, some games can resemble 'fun' drills, with the decision making reduced to substitution of a single word in a phrase. However, even in such cases, children are required to make individual choices based on specific language criteria which form part of the rules of the game. The key to a successful language game is that these rules are clear and the ultimate goal is well defined. Of course, the game must be fun, whether played in English or the children's mother tongue.

Integrating games into the syllabus

Although it would be conceivable to teach an English course solely based on games, most teachers have an accompanying textbook which they are required to work through over the course of the year. Games can either supplement the core material or (depending on the flexibility of the programme) replace activities which you dislike or feel uncomfortable with.

It is important for you to read your coursebooks or syllabus closely. Are there certain areas which appear weak? Perhaps there are aspects of the language (often functions) which are not covered in the core curriculum. A game can fill the gap. If your syllabus is based on language structures, the topic-based games in this book can make it more interesting for children.

But, most important, games can make your lesson planning easier. Once you have played the games a few times and feel comfortable with them, you will be able to insert them into your programme with very little preparation, especially if you have made materials which can be used more than once. Games can serve as a valuable backup if you go through your material too quickly or if something unexpected happens, for example, your colleague is ill and you need to cover her class as well as yours. They can help you control the rhythm of your lesson and get a group of unmotivated children up and moving around, participating in your class, and being more receptive to the rest of the lesson.

You can use language games to introduce new material, to practise recently learnt language items, to introduce or practise certain themes, or to relax or energize a class. Some can be used for all of these. Be very clear about what you expect of the children. The language focus alone is not enough to decide on a game. Consider the children's active and passive language knowledge in relation to what the game requires. Are full sentences or one-word answers sufficient? How strict are the contexts? Is there a large amount of choice for the children or are the responses closely defined? Do the games require active language production or simply passive understanding?

How you use a language game will ultimately depend on the 'personality' of the group of children. Do the children have a long attention span? Are they very active? What is the boy/girl ratio? (Sometimes girls and boys will refuse to play on the same team or to hold hands.) Also consider external factors such as the time of day the English lesson is held, and what happens before and after it. Is your lesson a part of the regular school day, or is it held in the late afternoon after a long day of school, homework, and other activities? Remember, too, to distinguish between 'rousing' and 'settling' games.

'Rousers' wake a class up. They get the adrenalin going. Typical 'rousers' are movement games and games where there is an element of competition. Guessing games also tend to get children excited, as do games which require the children to speak. Bear in mind that an active game may get excess energy out of one group and actually settle them. However, it could backfire and excite another group so much that they go wild and lose all control.

'Settlers', on the other hand, calm a class down. Typical 'settlers' are craft activities and games which focus on listening. Writing games also tend to settle a class, unless, of course, they are combined with other stirring elements, for example, running to the blackboard. Board games can settle a group as well.

The difference between 'rousers' and 'settlers' is not always clear. It depends on how you decide to play the game. Splitting a large group into pairs can make a 'rouser' into a 'settler', and can prevent children who are waiting for their turn from getting bored.

Before choosing a game, you should also consider safety. Is the space big enough for a lively movement game? Can the children fall and injure themselves? Is the floor dirty and not fit for sitting on?

Safety is also a matter of control. The children must know their boundaries and respect your authority. If a class is particularly unruly you should consider leaving out activities which could lead to pushing or throwing objects. These are really questions of common sense.

Here are some other basic points you may want to consider.

A game must be more than just fun

Of course all language games should be fun, but always keep the language component at the forefront of your planning. This may seem obvious, but it is easy for lessons to become a string of 'highlights' which lack coherence and fail to take the children further. Try and keep the focus on some clearly recognizable objectives rather than jumping from theme to theme in order to introduce popular games.

Play different games from lesson to lesson

Vary your repertoire. Children will always ask for their old favourites, but don't give in. The children call for games they know because they are familiar. However, one can have too much even of a good thing. Therefore, don't overdo a game, especially since many of the games in this collection can be adapted for use with various themes and differing levels of ability. If a game is over-used on one level, it will be difficult to motivate the children to try it another way.

Vary the order in which you play games

While a certain amount of routine in a lesson is useful, since children like to know what's going on, too much predictability will stifle a class as much as playing the same game over and over again. Avoid the repetitive trap of song–drill–game–craft, song–drill–game–craft. Mix things up a bit. Surprise the children from time to time. Sketching out lessons as mind maps (see example) instead of linear progressions can help you move away from static lesson plans while keeping the focus of the lesson clearly in sight. In this way, you can insert the game when energy and understanding are at their best.

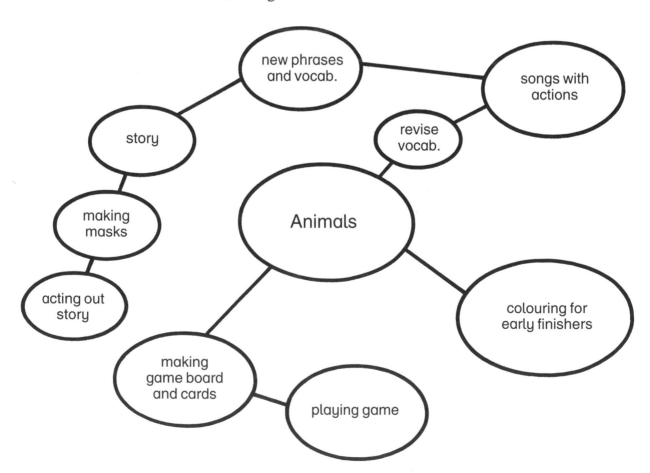

Always end an activity when the fun is still at its peak

It is very important not to play a game for too long. Children will begin to lose interest and wander off. Chaos may ensue.

Finding the right moment to switch activities is not easy. Each child has a different attention span. Therefore it is important that you have extra material for children who finish an activity quickly or who don't seem interested in continuing to play. Give them a job to do, like shuffling the cards or doing the calling for 'Bingo' (see 9.2). If a child still wants out, let him or her go. If a child is very unruly and disturbs the rest of the group you may also want to consider introducing a time-out chair, off to the side, where the child can go to calm down without losing touch with the group activity. Be careful when excluding a child in this way. The time-out chair can sometimes cause a child to play up to get attention, disturbing your game even more. So decide for each individual class and child.

Think ahead

The best-designed game will backfire if you are not fully sure about all aspects of the activity. Children are relentlessly honest critics who expect you, the teacher, to know everything. If you mix up the rules or get flustered, the children will rebel. The class can collapse in mayhem. With younger children you have no time to pause, rethink and reorganize as you might with classes of teenagers or young adults. To avoid such problems, test-play games yourself or with friends before introducing them into your English lesson.

Double check that you have everything you need. Note the 'Materials' heading for each game. If you have asked the children to bring materials, be sure to have a lot of extras yourself. Children will forget. Try and get into your classroom before the children arrive. Choose a table to one side and lay out everything you need before you start. Fishing for things in bags is a distraction which can lead to a loss of discipline—your eyes and attention are away from the children.

Finally, does the classroom space fit the requirements of the game you have chosen? Is the classroom full of chairs and tables? If so, can they be moved around? Is the space large enough to put objects around the room or for two teams to run in? If you have the opportunity to arrange the room in your own way, dividing it into a sitting area and an empty space, perhaps with a carpet to sit on, is a good idea. This way, you can move between activities without having to interrupt the flow of the lesson.

Making games into part of the syllabus

One of the best ways to get children interested in a game is to have them participate actively in its creation. Producing a game gives the children a sense of achievement while integrating the game into

Standard 'snake' track

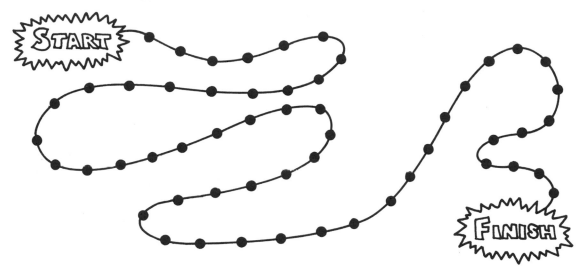

'Never-ending' track

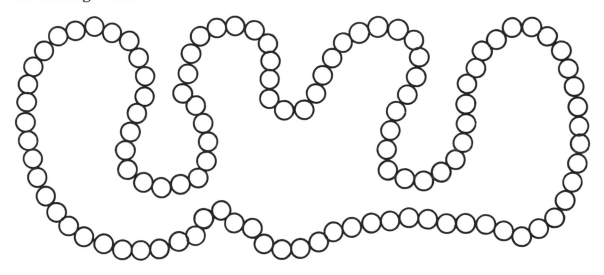

Multi-route track

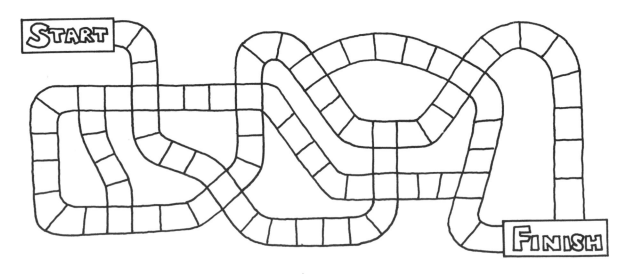

other areas of the language class and the children's general education. Game creation involves many skills as well as active decision making on the part of the children. It is a rich field in which to practise some basic English. For instance, in deciding rules for games, you could integrate phrases such as *How many* … (players, cards, turns) *What happens when* … (you land on a red space, roll a six, have no more cards) *Can you* … (roll twice with doubles, jump over another player). Depending on the children's language level, you can require full sentences in a loosely controlled context, or focus on passive understanding and answers with *yes/no* or single-word utterances. On the non-linguistic level, the rules can be as simple or hard as the children's general development and imagination allow.

Creating games is also an excellent craft activity and can involve a lot of language use. The children can make their own dice (they can have any set of symbols, not only numbers—see Worksheet 2.12 on page 139), create cards (you can make this into a listening task by telling the children what to draw), and, of course, design a game board based on rules they have already agreed upon. The game creation project can (should) stretch over a couple of lessons, but not too many, perhaps as a closing activity when concentration is low. Game making almost always excites the children. The project culminates on a special day when the game is played.

Language level

Determining a learner's language level is at best an inexact science, especially if the learner is a young child. Traditional terms such as beginner, intermediate, and advanced suggest a linear progression which is really not applicable to the 4–12 age group, as it is difficult to filter out the language component from children's general development. Children at pre-school and early primary level are meeting English for the first time. Most will probably not learn intensively. Some will start in kindergarten while others may only begin when they are ten years old. If traditional terminology is to fit at all, we would need to list 'pre-school beginners, early primary beginners, primary intermediate', etc., which would only make things more complex for a teacher looking for a suitable game.

We thought long and hard about whether to include language level in the details of each game and reached the conclusion that any attempt to classify the games in this way would be very artificial. Language level does not reflect the real challenge of the games, which you will find in the nature of the activity itself rather than in the language component. In addition, since most games have numerous variations with different language input aimed at varying age groups, giving a language level could lead readers to overlook activities which might be just what they need.

For these reasons language levels are not included. Instead, the games in each chapter are in order of age: from youngest to oldest. Use the indexes at the back of the book to help you choose a game suitable for your class.

Class size

Controlling large classes (25+ children) is one of the hardest tasks facing even the most experienced teacher. It is a simple fact of teaching life that the larger the group, the more difficult it becomes to set up activities which promote active language use. You can play some games with large classes, especially those based on total physical response, such as line-ups, 'Simon Says', but they tend to elicit passive responses to prompts. Giving the teacher's role to the children can counterbalance this to some extent, but the shortcomings of the large class still remain.

Rather than spending time looking for activities which allow for 25 and more children to participate simultaneously, it is best to divide a class up into smaller, more manageable groups which can play games more effectively. Here are some ideas which have worked for teachers we know.

Turn players into teams

If you have a game which is suitable for eight players, you can expand it to 24 players by playing in groups of three. Try and encourage English as the means of communication between team members (this can be difficult) and *insist* that one player from each team (a different child each time) *must* produce the target language. You could also get each team to respond in chorus if the game permits.

Set up 'game stations' in the classroom

'Game stations' enable groups of children to play different games at the same time. Set up everything you need for each game in a different part of the room. The stations should be clearly marked with bright and colourful signs which the children can make. Split the class into four groups (4 x 10 children, for example) and assign them each to a station where they should play a game. Take care to ensure that the games do not interfere with each other. Depending on the space available, loud lively games could disturb children working on something quiet. In all cases you should make sure that:

- the games are familiar in concept to the children. You can vary the language components.
- the children move briskly from station to station, spending no more than 10–15 minutes at each, and less for the very young, who may require further guidance.

There needn't only be games at each station. Set up a book station with lots of interesting picture books to look at or read, a listening station with a tape-player for listening to songs or stories, a computer station if available, and a game station. You can also create a 'teacher station' where the children can come and speak to you.

You and a few children should demonstrate a game to the whole class, after which the class splits into groups to play. Circulate from group to group acting as a monitor and source of information.

The beauty of the 'stations' idea is that once it has been explained and practised it can easily be modified for use with any topic. The children will know what to expect, making classroom management easier.

Dealing with children who are 'out' of games

Many games have winners and losers and often losers are 'out' of the game. Also, in non-competitive games, some children may simply finish quicker than others. These children need to be occupied in case they wander off and disrupt those still playing. Two interesting strategies are:

A 'consolation' round

Split the class into small groups to play the game. Rather than being 'out', losers from one group go on to compete with the losers from another group. They can either play a new round of the same game or move into a completely different game, running parallel to the first one. In this way the stigma of losing is reduced and an interest in the game is maintained even after a child is 'out'. (Who and what will I play next?) The same principle can be applied in the opposite direction. Winners can also go on to play other winners, or the winners of game A play the losers of game B. In this way no one is ever 'out'—each team or player gets another chance.

The central game board

On a large sheet of cardboard create a bright and colourful game board. (See the games in this book for ideas, or get ideas from your class.) Children who are 'out' roll the dice and move across the board, landing on different spaces. Each space represents a particular activity or game which the children must play. Some spaces can tell the children to take a card with instructions written on it which they must read and carry out. (With pre-schoolers, you need to explain instead.) The children go off and play that game. When they finish, they return to the game board, roll the dice and move on to something new.

A word on the mother tongue

The games in this book do not require mother-tongue explanation if they are introduced systematically, with simple games coming first. The more complex games will build on the easier ones. This is important if you have a multilingual class.

Nevertheless, there are times when a mother-tongue explanation can be helpful. This is especially true if you want to play a more complicated game with younger children, or if you want to use a game which includes concepts and procedures the children have not yet learnt.

If you start explaining a game in English and realize the class simply does not understand what you mean, a short prompt in the mother tongue will get you over the hurdle and on to the game in question. Resolutely sticking to English regardless of the situation will test the children's patience and spell trouble for classroom management. Take note of what the children didn't understand and try and introduce the game differently the next time around.

It is inevitable and logical that young children will speak in their mother tongue during a lesson. Pre-school and primary-age children seldom have enough English to communicate freely with their classmates. And why should they if their friends speak the same language? Be aware of the distinction between the target English you should require in the lesson and the off-task mother-tongue talking that will take place. While you should encourage the children to use English amongst themselves, don't press the issue. The more the children learn, the broader the use of the target language becomes.

What is important is that *you* stick to English as much as possible. If a child addresses you in the mother tongue, it is fine to acknowledge the question, but respond in English. You may even want to tease some English out of the children by responding to a mother-tongue question with: *Sorry? Could you say that in English? I don't speak …* etc., and using gestures.

Useful game-playing terms

Here are some phrases which are essential to playing games. When you first play games with your class be sure to demonstrate the meaning of phrases while saying them. Before you start the game let each child have a turn at saying the phrase. The children will pick it up very fast. You may have to remind them in the next lesson, but after a brief warm-up, the phrases will come back quickly.

It's my/your/her turn
Whose turn is it?
You're out
Roll the dice

Shuffle the cards
Take …
Give …
Wait …
Don't peek (look)
No cheating
Move … spaces forward/backwards
Make a circle
Line up
Turn around
Shut your eyes
Pass the (ball, cup, etc.)
Spin the …
Discard (throw away)
Deal the cards.

Essential materials

It is a good idea to build up a stock of picture cards showing people, food, common classroom and household objects, animals, etc. Some examples are given in the Flashcards on pages 142–5, but you can also collect pictures from magazines etc. and stick them to card.

Although the materials you need are listed with each game, here is a list of core materials which you should collect and always have handy in the primary classroom.

large thick cardboard sheets (such as A1 size) to make game boards (coloured and white)
small cards such as index cards
coloured pencils and pens (washable)
children's scissors
children's glue
Blu-tack (This is a kind of putty which you can use to stick paper or small objects to walls or boards without ripping the material. Blu-tack or its equivalent is not available everywhere and simple tape will do the trick as well.)
lots of colourful magazines (preferably in English but others will do as well—it's the pictures we need)
lots of dice, as varied as possible (can be found in speciality and toy shops)
small toys or figures to be used as counters
dried beans
old clothes
egg cartons
scrap paper
a soft ball for indoor use
a stop-watch
a whistle
a buzzer.

How to use this book

How this book is organized

Chapter headings: themes

The games in this book are arranged according to areas which are central to a young child's experience: themes with which they can immediately identify regardless of language. The order of themes is not random but grows from a central point: the children themselves. Each wider theme contains the information from the theme before, used in a different, exciting way. Thus, although 'colours' as a theme appears early on in the book, the reader will find games with colours in many other areas as well.

You can use many games with more than one theme, and themes themselves often overlap. The choices made in this book reflect our own classroom experiences and should serve as a guide, not a dogma. Draw your own conclusions about where a game fits in best, in the light of your own circumstances.

A thematic approach does not mean that we concentrate only on vocabulary. All too often we see children who can recite any number of nouns, but are incapable of putting together a functioning sentence, phrase, or even a simple utterance. Unfortunately, producing a lot of individual words looks good at parents' meetings but does not show a child how to *communicate* in English. Some games require only single-word responses to prompts, but we try to place these in broader communicative contexts, offering children small, easily digestible patterns of English which convey meaning above and beyond the identification of an object. The variations and comments on the individual games give useful tips for expanding language use.

Game type

It is important to know what types of game are available in order to plan a lesson with a balanced rhythm. There are many different types of games: card games, board games, movement games, games with music, to name but a few. However, many games are difficult to label. Therefore, we have assigned a each game a type based on its most outstanding feature—for example, although a board game includes dice rolling, the board itself is the primary focus.

Movement games
In these games, the children are physically active. Movement games are generally 'rousers' and need to be closely monitored.

Card games

Children collect, give away, exchange, sort, and count cards. The cards can have a meaning or value in a game, or simply serve as symbols for objects or actions. (It is unlikely that you will have an elephant handy and it is not easy to describe snow-skiing in a tropical country.) Cards are often components of other game types as well.

Board games

Any games which mainly involve moving markers along a path. Board games can be made by the children as a fun craft activity.

Dice games

Dice games are incredibly versatile. Remember that the dice need not only have numbers on the faces. They can have numbers, colours, letters of the alphabet—virtually anything you like. Dice need not be six-sided either. In speciality shops you can find 12-sided dice or even round dice with a weighted ball in the middle. Little children might only roll one dice, while older children can play games with three or four dice at the same time. A dice template is provided in Worksheet 2.12 (page 139); you and your children can also make spinners (pages 107–8).

Drawing games

Drawing games are special because they span a gap between key functions of the brain. On the one hand, drawing requires creativity and a sensitivity towards the world. On the other hand, the children must be able to understand instructions and describe their art. Drawing games are particularly helpful with shy children who are reluctant to talk. A picture is a very personal thing and although children may not be ready to describe their picture, they will certainly respond to your questions with *yes* or *no* answers.

Guessing games

In guessing games, the aim is to guess the answer to a question of some kind.

Role-play games

Role-play games can be seen as simple, guided drama activities. The language input can be quite rigidly prescribed or very open depending on the language level, curiosity, and confidence of your class. Role plays stimulate a child's imagination and are tests of true communication.

Singing and chanting games

Singing and chanting games often involve movement, but we decided to list them separately since music plays such an important role in early childhood learning.

Team games

Team games can belong to the other categories, but also require co-operative team work.

Word games

These games utilize children's enjoyment of playing with words. They are mostly for older children as they involve spelling and writing.

Aims

Language

This heading gives guidance on the English you can teach or practise in the game. The list of language items is by no means all inclusive. While some of the games are strictly linked with specific language, many others are flexible and their language can vary according to your needs. Often there are further possibilities under the heading 'Variations'.

Other

Language learning cannot be divorced from child development as a whole. It makes no sense to introduce a game requiring simple addition if the children can't count. Nor would a directional game work with children who do not know left from right. Where games require or develop clear, specific, non-linguistic skills, they are listed under this heading. If no non-linguistic skills are listed, you should nevertheless be familiar with the general stage of development of children at that age. You should learn as much as you can about child development as a whole, and the curriculum in your country or region, for example, when do children begin reading and writing?

For teachers new to the primary classroom it is very important to be aware of what a child at a particular age is capable of understanding and doing, both mentally and physically.

– Can the children identify numbers out of sequence?
– Can they tell the time?
– Does a game require hand–eye co-ordination?
– Should the children be able to read?

Many of the games actively develop important non-linguistic skills; for example, several games encourage children to think in categories, to observe and recognize, and to group and match objects and actions according to specific features. Of course, all the games encourage children to learn to stick to the rules and co-operate. See the Index on page 149.

Age

This is a recommendation and guideline for teachers, not a rule. Please bear in mind that age is only a relative indicator of child development. Some three-year-olds can be more advanced than some five-year-olds. Also, if older children are absolute beginners, they will need and enjoy simpler games at first.

Group size

The minimum and maximum recommended number of children needed to play a game successfully. Remember that group size is not the same as class size. Large classes can be split into smaller groups which play the game simultaneously, after an initial demonstration by the teacher for all the children.

Time

Average playing time for each game. If the class is large or small, the time may be shorter or longer.

Materials

A list of items (if any) needed to play the game.

Description

A short paragraph to explain the object of more complicated games.

Preparation

What you need to do before playing a game, including setting it up and preparing materials. Some boards and cards may take some time to make, but picture cards, etc. will be useful for many games and activities, again and again. Often the children can help to make them as a craft activity.

It is important to teach any new language needed before the game starts.

Procedure

A step-by-step description of how to play the game.

Variations

These are ideas for expanding or adapting the main game for other themes, language, or age groups. Variations may also simply be new twists on the original game, making it more interesting to children who have played it before, or perhaps making it a bit more difficult.

Comments

Any other important points which do not fit into the other categories.

Choosing language games

Indexes

At the end of the book there are indexes of games by type, language, and non-linguistic skills, to help you find a game suitable for a particular lesson. Once you have used these to narrow down your selection, read the games and their variations, and pick what is right for you and your children. Improvise a bit. Don't feel compelled to follow our instructions word for word. Although a game for 4–6-year-olds might not suit your 10-year-olds, it could inspire you to develop something new that would.

And now, on to the games. Be creative. Experiment a bit. But above all, have fun!

1 Family, friends, and me

Family and friends are a child's first and most intimate point of identification. Children feel safe and secure among family and friends. They are a solid base from which to venture forth into something new and 'foreign'.

It is also a logical point of departure from your perspective as a teacher. Starting off with *Family, friends, and me* will help you get to know your children. You will learn important details which will help you customize your later lessons. Of course, the children will learn a lot about each other as well. Starting off with this theme requires immediate interaction and communication. Language is personalized and realistic from the start.

While naturally introducing basic family vocabulary, the games in this section also focus on greetings, introductions, and question words.

1.1 Hello game

GAME TYPE	**Movement game**
AIMS	**Language:** Names; basic introductions and greetings.
AGE	**4+**
GROUP SIZE	**6–15**
TIME	**10 minutes**
MATERIALS	A drum, whistle, or other noise-maker; a soft ball (Follow-up 1).

PROCEDURE

1 All the children sit on chairs in a circle. You are in the middle.
2 Go up to a child, shake hands, and say *Hello, my name is …*
3 You and the child now introduce yourselves to other children. Then they stand up and introduce themselves to other children.
4 When all the children are up and moving about make a noise with your drum or whistle. You and the children must run and find a seat. There will be one seat too few.
5 The child who doesn't find a seat goes to the middle and starts the game again. You sit on a seat like the other children.

FOLLOW-UP 1

After they have introduced themselves, the children sit in a circle and one throws a soft ball to another, who has to say *Hello, I'm …*

FOLLOW-UP 2	Child 1 throws the ball to Child 2, calling out Child 2's name. Child 2 says *Hello ..., how are you?* They then change places.
VARIATION 1	Instead of *Hello*, you can choose *Good morning* or *Good afternoon*.
VARIATION 2	Instead of *My name is ...* use *I'm ...*
VARIATION 3	The children have to answer *It's nice to meet you* or *My pleasure*. After each round, the child in the middle can introduce new phrases: for example, *I'm six years old* or *I live in Rome*.

1.2   Through the peephole

GAME TYPE	**Guessing game**
AIMS	**Language:** *Who is it? Is it ...? Yes, it is/No it isn't*; possessive *-'s*. **Other:** Observation.
AGE	4–10
GROUP SIZE	8–10
TIME	**10 minutes**
MATERIALS	Photographs of the children and their families, or common objects; five sheets of cardboard with progressively larger peepholes cut in the middle of each (the sheets can be decorated by the children).
PREPARATION	Ask the children to bring in photographs of their families.
PROCEDURE	1 Each child introduces his or her family by showing the photographs and pointing, saying, *This is my Dad*, etc.

2 Choose a picture. Don't let the children see it. Place the five sheets of cardboard over the picture. Have the sheet with the largest hole on the bottom and the smallest on the top. The children sit in a circle around the sheets.

3 Let the children peer through the little peephole. They will see a small section of the photograph or picture. Ask them *Who is it?* The children guess. For the very young, one-word responses are enough; otherwise, the children use the phrase *Is it ...?* They must not guess at pictures of their own families.

4 All the children concentrate on trying to remember the appearances of the other children's families. Older children can use the possessive, for example, *This is Tom's sister*.

5 If the children cannot guess who the picture is, remove the top sheet. The hole is bigger now. Ask them *Can you guess who it is now?* The children guess.

6 Continue removing sheets until the children guess correctly or the picture is completely revealed.

VARIATION 1	If you want to make the game more competitive, divide the group into two teams. Award dried beans or counters as points.
VARIATION 2	Let the first child to guess the picture choose the next one and take the teacher's role, answering questions and removing the sheets.
VARIATION 3	You can also use pictures of common objects. For older children, you can use pictures of famous people.
COMMENTS	**1** It's up to you to decide how much language the children should produce. You can drill individual words but also insist that the children respond in phrases.
	2 Keep the groups small so that the children can see.

1.3 Zip-zap!

GAME TYPE	**Movement game**
AIMS	**Language:** *What's your name? His/Her name is … .* **Other:** Group dynamics; memory training; left/right co-ordination; quick reactions.
AGE	**6+**
GROUP SIZE	**8–30**
TIME	**10 minutes**
MATERIALS	(for Variation 1) A soft ball or a bean bag.
PROCEDURE	**1** The children sit on chairs in a circle. There are no empty chairs.
	2 Stand in the middle. Point to a child and say either *Zip!* or *Zap!*
	3 When you say *Zip!* the child you are pointing to says the name of the child sitting to his or her left, for example, *Her name is Jane.* When you say *Zap!* the child you are pointing to says the name of the child sitting to his or her right.
	4 Once the children get used to the game, keep the pace fast. After a while, instead of pointing to a child, call *Zip-Zap!* Now all the children stand up and run to a different chair.
	5 The children quickly find out the names of their new neighbours. Check that the children ask each other in English. Allow only a short time for this. Then point again and say *Zip!* or *Zap!*
	6 After three or four rounds, call *Zip-Zap!* and sit down on a free chair too. This leaves one child without a chair. He or she takes over your role by pointing and saying *Zip!*, *Zap!* or *Zip-Zap!*

VARIATION 1	Instead of pointing, throw a small soft ball or a bean bag.
VARIATION 2	Instead of using the terms *Zip!* and *Zap!* say *Left* or *Right* or ask questions, for example, *Who's on your left?*
FOLLOW-UP	Once the children know each other's names well, change the criteria to age, eye/hair colour, likes/dislikes, etc.
COMMENTS	This is ideal for a new class who do not yet know each other's names.

1.4 Names chant

GAME TYPE	**Chanting game**
AIMS	**Language:** *My/Your name's* …; sentence stress. **Other:** Keeping rhythm.
AGE	6+
GROUP SIZE	6–30
TIME	**10 minutes**
PROCEDURE	1 The children sit on chairs in a circle. The object of the game is for the children to say their own name and the name of another child, keeping to a strict chanting rhythm and speed. 2 Begin the chant by clapping your hands, first on your thighs (*one*), then together (*two*), then clicking the fingers of your right hand (*three*) and then your left hand (*four*) so that a rhythm of four beats

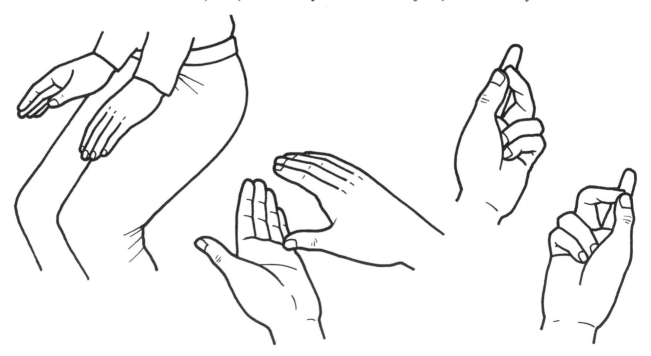

is clearly audible and visible. The first few times, count *one*, *two*, *three*, *four* so that the rhythm is clear to all the children.

3 The children copy these actions all together. Once they have got used to this, say your own name on beat three and the name of a child on beat four.

4 The child whose name you called says his or her own name on beat three and the name of another child on beat four. Thus the chant is passed from child to child.

5 After a while, extend the chant to the phrase *My name's …* (on beats one and two) and *Your name's …* (on beats three and four). Using this kind of phrase in a chanting game increases the language used, but it is rather challenging and requires practice.

VARIATION 1

Change the phrases used in this chant as you like. However, be aware that they should always fit into a four-beat rhythm. The second phrase must always give clear information of who is meant to go next, otherwise there will be confusion.

VARIATION 2

Try using a three- or six-beat rhythm with different actions and phrases. It's worth experimenting as children love this kind of chanting game.

1.5 Identity swap

GAME TYPE

Role-play game

AIMS

Language: Introductions; *What's your name? My name is …*; question words: *What, Where, How*.

AGE

7+ (4+ for Variation 1)

GROUP SIZE

8–15

TIME

10–15 minutes

MATERIALS

(for Variation 3) Identity cards.

PROCEDURE

1 The children stand in the centre of the room. Step towards one child and introduce yourself, for example, *My name is Superman. I'm ten.*

2 The child introduces him- or herself to you in the same way: *My name is Roberta. I'm seven.*

3 Move to another child and introduce yourself as the first child: *My name is Roberta. I'm seven.*

4 The first child introduces him- or herself to another child with your name: *My name is Superman. I'm ten.*

5 All the children mix and continue to introduce themselves, using the name of the child they have just met. Monitor the short conversations to keep them on track.

6 After about 5–7 minutes tell the children to stop.

7 Ask all the children to introduce themselves to the group with their new identities.

VARIATION 1

Give very young children the names of colours or animals. They need only say *I'm ...* and swap the noun.

VARIATION 2

With more advanced children expand the simple introductions to include other question-and-answer pairs such as *How old are you? I'm ... Where do you live? I live in ... What's your telephone number?*

VARIATION 3

Make identity cards which the children choose from a pile and exchange after introducing themselves. The children can make these cards under your guidance as a picture dictation type of exercise.

1.6   Blind date

GAME TYPE

Guessing game

AIMS

Language: Asking and answering questions.
Other: Recognition.

AGE

8+

GROUP SIZE

6–12

TIME

15–20 minutes

MATERIALS

A blindfold; scoreboard.

DESCRIPTION

A 'blind date' is a meeting between two people who have never seen each other before. This game makes use of blindfolds to create a similar situation, although children in any class will of course know each other. The object of the game is to guess the name of another child, by asking questions, listening carefully to the answers, and recognizing the voice.

PROCEDURE

1 The children sit in a line at one end of the room. Blindfold the first child, who stands a few metres away from the other children.

2 Choose another child to be the 'blind date'. He or she stands opposite the blindfolded child at a distance of about two metres. During the game, all the other players must be silent!

3 The blindfolded child now asks the blind date questions, for example *How old are you? Have you got a brother? Have you got brown hair? Can you swim? Do you like apples?*

4 The 'blind date' child answers, trying to change the sound of his or her voice (for example, making it higher or lower) and as briefly as possible. The blindfolded child tries to recognize the voice.

5 Once the blindfolded child knows who the 'blind date' is, he or she asks *Is your name …?* or *Are you …?* If the guess is correct, the child gets five points. The 'blind date' child gets one point for each answer he or she gives without being recognized. The game continues until every child has been blindfolded and played the role of 'blind date' once.

VARIATION 1	Simplify the game and use it as a names-learning game right at the beginning of the course. The blindfolded child says only *Hello!* Or a very short dialogue can be practised, such as *How are you? I'm fine, thank you.*
VARIATION 2	Instead of one child asking the questions, have the whole group say clues such as *She's got brown hair.*
VARIATION 3	If there is a danger that children who are waiting for their turn get bored, make it into a team game, so that those children encourage their team. Be strict about refereeing this version, as a team should not give away the name of the blind date.
COMMENTS	Children who know each other well will not easily be fooled by a disguised voice. Have another child answer questions for the blind date.

1.7 Family ties

GAME TYPE	**Team game**
AIMS	**Language:** Possessives. **Other:** Understanding family relationships.
AGE	7+
GROUP SIZE	8–16
TIME	**20 minutes**
MATERIALS	A large piece of cardboard and several smaller coloured cards; felt-tip pens to draw or magazines to cut out pictures; scissors; a loud buzzer or alarm; Blu-tack or sellotape to stick the cards to the board.
PREPARATION	Before class make a large family tree to display. (See the example on page 28.) If your class is very large or you have no overhead projector, make an identical family tree for each team and one for yourself to use as a guide. The children could make these in earlier lessons.

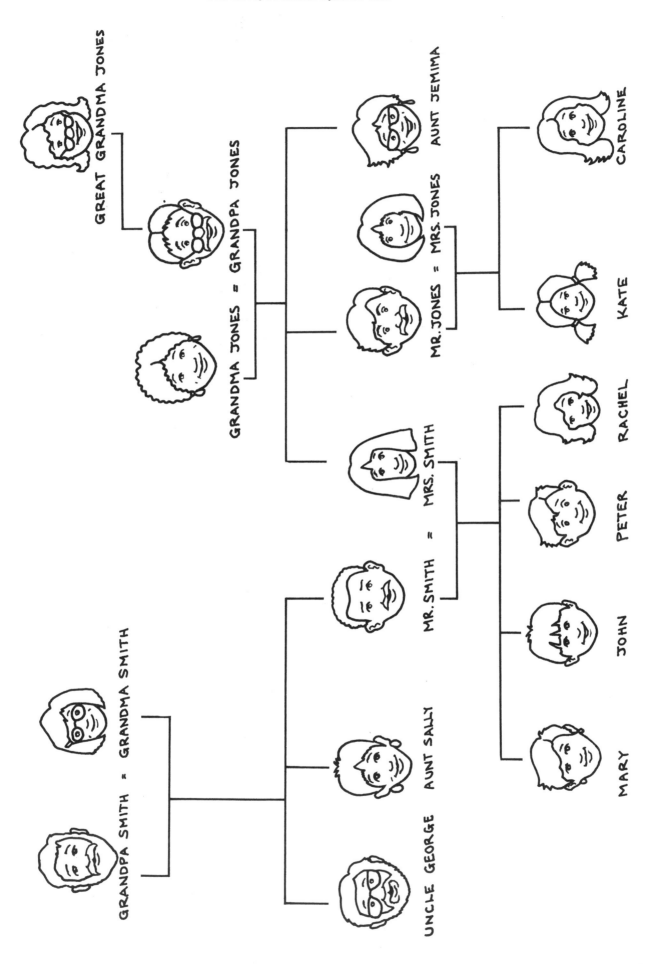

PROCEDURE

1 Point to and explain a few family relationships, for example *Joe is Martha's brother. Mr Wiley is Christina's father.* The structures and vocabulary should be familiar to the children from previous lessons. Be patient—it may take a little while for them to understand.

2 Split the class into two teams, or two sets of two teams in a large class.

3 Point to two pictures on the family tree.

4 The first team tries to explain the relationship. If they make a language mistake, such as *John is the brother from Jane* or *Liz Amy mother*, or leaving out prepositions altogether, or simply get the relationship wrong, sound your alarm or buzzer.

5 The opposing team now has a chance to give the correct answer and earn one point. Whether they answer correctly or not, the next question goes to the second team.

6 When all children in each team have had a turn, the team with the most points wins.

VARIATION 1

Once the children understand this game well, get them to point for the opposing team.

VARIATION 2

Put the alarm in the middle. If a team makes a mistake, the other team sounds the alarm. If it wasn't a mistake the team which was right gets an extra point.

VARIATION 3

Add occupations, for example, *Martha is the daughter of the baker. Mr Smith's son is a student.*

VARIATION 4

The children could make family trees of their own families. Be aware, however, of single-parent children, orphans, etc. who might feel embarrassed about doing this.

COMMENTS

You may want to consider awarding different points for content and language mistakes.

1.8 Uniting families

GAME TYPE — **Card and movement game**

AIMS — **Language:** *Who are you? I'm … father, mother, brother, sister, son, daughter.*
Other: Understanding family relationships.

AGE — 6+

GROUP SIZE — 12–24 (must be divisible by four)

TIME — **10–15 minutes**

| MATERIALS | Cards with names and/or pictures of family members, one card per child—each family has four members (except Variation 2); music. |

PROCEDURE

1 Mix the cards and give one to each child. Explain to them that each card is a member of a family.
2 Play some music. The children move through the room exchanging cards with each other.
3 Stop the music after a short time. Tell the children that they must find the rest of their family. They cannot look at other players' cards but must ask questions such as *Who are you?* The child can then answer *I'm Father Smith* or *Son Jones*, etc.
4 When the children think they have found all the members of their family, they sit down at a table and call out *Ready*.
5 Play stops and the children must describe who they are. If they are right, they win.

VARIATION 1

Instead of giving the families names, give them symbols (hearts, stars, moons, suns, etc.) which the children are familiar with. You can also colour code the families.

VARIATION 2

Expand the vocabulary to include wider family members: aunts, uncles, cousins, grandparents. In this case reduce the number of families.

COMMENTS

Children can be rather rough when they exchange their cards. Although this part of the activity should be fun, set clear rules for the children's behaviour (no pushing or screaming, etc.).

1.9 Family tree

GAME TYPE   **Board game**

AIMS   **Language:** Present simple tense; possessive -'s.

AGE   **8+**

GROUP SIZE   **4–8**

TIME   **20 minutes**

MATERIALS   A large board for every 4–8 players showing a family tree (see the example on page 31); a set of small cards with pictures and written descriptions of people in various jobs (see the Flashcards on page 145); a small toy or any other marker; dice; plastic counters.

PREPARATION   Make the board and cards. They can be kept for future games. For clarity, the joining lines should be arrows, pointing in the direction of movement around the board, which makes it into a track board game.

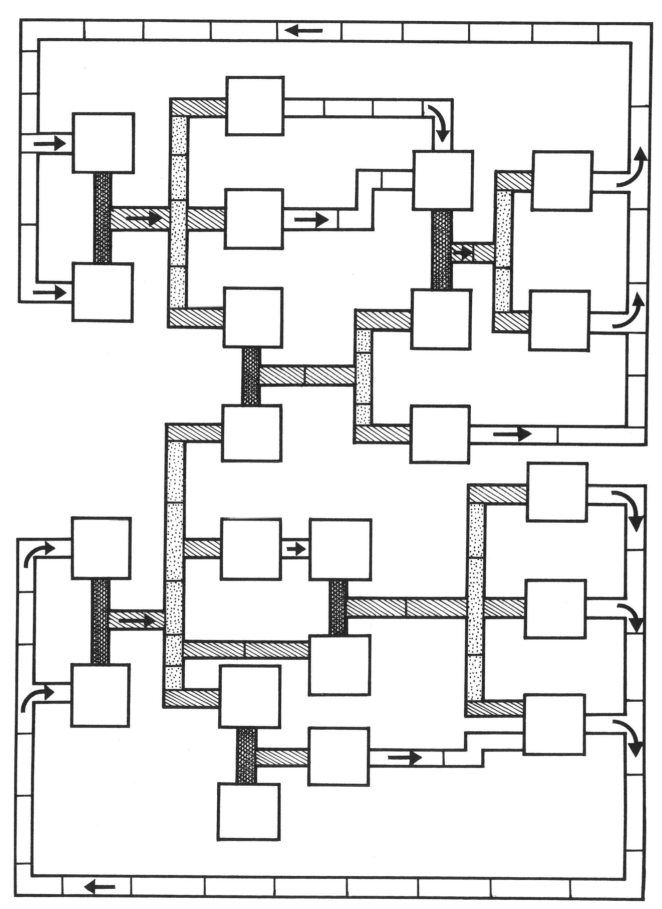

PROCEDURE

1 Shuffle the cards well and distribute them randomly face up on the family tree. Place the marker on any card. The object of the game is to describe the members of the family tree.

2 In turn, the children roll the dice and move the marker around the family tree. The marker may only move along the joining lines. Each child describes the person on the family tree where the marker lands. They have to say up to three things about that person, for example, *The doctor is the policeman's son. He's got three children. His mother is a secretary.* The information must be true and available from the board.

3 For each correct sentence the children get a point. Set a time limit of, say, 30 seconds for each description. The children may describe any particular card only once. Mark it with a small plastic counter so that everyone can see that it has already been described.

4 When all the people on the family tree have been described, the child with the most points wins. You can also set a time limit (say 15 minutes) and total the scores at this time.

VARIATION 1

Allow the children to add additional information to their descriptions with phrases they know, such as *He likes chocolate. His name is Peter. He's 26 years old. He can swim.* Allow more time for this (40–60 seconds). The children get a point for each plausible, grammatically correct sentence.

VARIATION 2

Instead of using plastic counters to mark the characters, turn the cards over. The children have to try to memorize the characters and their positions on the family tree. Referee this version strictly, checking each time that the information given was correct.

VARIATION 3

The children say one 'true' and one 'false' statement about the person they are describing. The other children correct the false statement.

1.10   Picture identity cards

GAME TYPE	**Board game**
AIMS	**Language:** Describing people.
AGE	8+
GROUP SIZE	4–8
TIME	**20–25 minutes**
MATERIALS	A simple 'snake-track' board; dice; counters; 20–30 cards with pictures of various people.

PREPARATION

1 Together with the children draw a 'snake-track', which is a simple long line with a start and a finish, on a large board. Make one for every 4–8 children. Along the line draw black dots (about 50) and colour every seventh dot red. Put the counters at the start, one for each child. The object of the game is to be the first player to reach the finish.

2 Make 20–30 picture cards with people on for each group. You can use magazine pictures or the children can draw them.

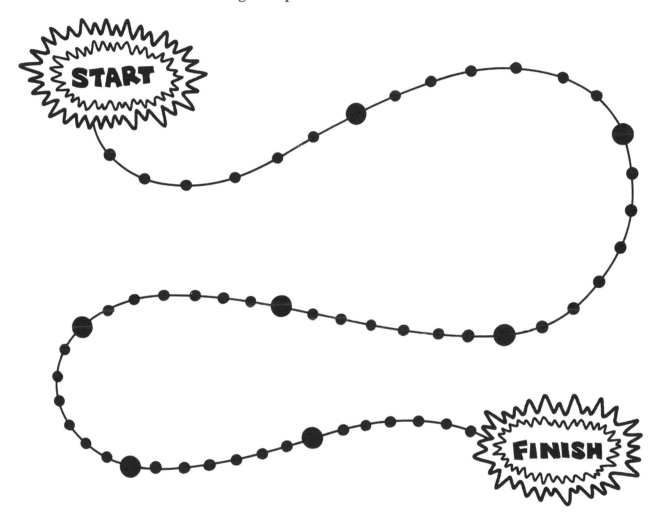

PROCEDURE

1 Put the children into groups of 4–8. In turn, the children roll the dice and move their counters along the track.

2 If a child lands on a red dot, he or she takes a card and turns it face up for everyone to see. The child then describes the person on the card, giving as many details as possible, for example, *This is a man. He's 43 years old. He's got brown eyes and short hair. He's wearing jeans and a T-shirt.* The child may move his or her counter one dot forward for every correct sentence. Allow a maximum of five sentences per person. If the child makes a mistake, he or she must move his or her counter one dot back.

3 The game is over when a player has reached the finish or when all the cards have been described.

2 Numbers

Numbers are universal. Virtually anything can be counted. They are a theme which will constantly reappear in every other aspect of language you teach. Numbers are such a common part of everybody's experience that they are almost not a theme in the traditional sense. Numbers are a general concept which can be applied again and again to almost every aspect of life.

It is because of this universality and versatility that we recommend teaching numbers very early on in a course. If your children have a firm understanding of numbers you will have far more options in choosing activities in other language areas as well.

Games in this chapter focus on functions such as counting, simple addition, and subtraction, as well as the sub-theme telling the time. Some key structures are *How many/much? Is there/Are there?* and *Have got.*

2.1 Bean toss

GAME TYPE	**Movement game**
AIMS	**Language:** Revising numbers. **Other:** Recognition of number symbols; throwing accurately.
AGE	4+
GROUP SIZE	4–8
TIME	**5 minutes**
MATERIALS	Beans; egg cartons; (for Variation 3) bean bags; paper plates; balls; buckets.
PREPARATION	Prepare an egg carton by writing the numbers 1–6, 1–10 or 1–12, depending on the size of the cartons and the children's knowledge of numbers, in each hole. Place the egg carton at one end of the room.
PROCEDURE	1 Show the children how to throw the beans into the egg carton. The distance to the target will depend on the size and throwing abilities of the children. The number of beans should be the same as the highest number in the egg carton.
	2 In turn, the children throw the beans, one by one, into the target. Keep the pace fast, so there are no long waits.

3 Once children have thrown all their beans, they count out the number of beans which landed in the egg carton. Then they place the beans in the right hole. For example, if a child gets five beans into the egg carton, he or she puts them in the hole with the number five. Check that this is right. The child then collects all the beans and gives them to the next child.

VARIATION 1	The children collect the beans which missed the target and count these, putting them in the right hole.
VARIATION 2	Make the game competitive by awarding a point for each bean which lands in a hole.
VARIATION 3	This game can also be played on a much larger scale with balls and buckets or bean bags and paper plates.
COMMENTS	Strict control over the bean throwing is vital to maintain order in this game. With very young children it is important to watch that they don't try to eat the beans.

2.2 Big foot

GAME TYPE	**Movement game**
AIMS	**Language:** Counting. **Other:** Balance; co-ordination.
AGE	**4–9**
GROUP SIZE	**4–10**
TIME	**5 minutes**
MATERIALS	Thick cardboard; pens; Blu-tack or sticky tape.
PREPARATION	Ideally, you should prepare two or three large stencils of footprints which the children can draw around. Then, together with the children draw and cut out ten large footprints from thick cardboard. Stick the footprints on the floor in one direction, as if a monster has walked through the room and left a trail. You could also draw the footprints on the ground with chalk.
PROCEDURE	In turn, the children hop or jump along the trail, counting each step.
VARIATION 1	If a child misses a footprint or his or her foot goes over the edge, he or she has to go back to the start.
VARIATION 2	Make the game competitive, either by timing the children or by using two trails with two children competing. Referee this version strictly.

| **VARIATION 3** | The children count backwards from 10 down to 1. |

| **VARIATION 4** | Write the numbers on the footprints. The children not hopping or jumping can count alongside the active child. |

| **VARIATION 5** | Extend the track of footprints to practise counting higher numbers (for example, 1–12 or 1–20). The children can also count in multiples of two, three, five, or ten. |

| **VARIATION 6** | With older children, if a child steps over the side of one of the footprints, he or she may only continue along the track if he or she answers a question correctly. |

2.3   Magic matchbox

| **GAME TYPE** | **Guessing game** |

| **AIMS** | **Language:** *Is/are there …? Yes, there is/are. No, there isn't/aren't.* |

| **AGE** | **4+** |

| **GROUP SIZE** | **4–10** |

| **TIME** | **5–10 minutes** |

| **MATERIALS** | A matchbox; a lot of spent matches; marbles, pebbles, etc.; flashcards of words to revise; (for Variation 2) a hat. |

| **DESCRIPTION** | The object of the game is to acquire as many matches as possible. |

| **PREPARATION** | Hide a secret number of matches in the matchbox, but remember exactly how many. |

| **PROCEDURE** | 1 Put a large pile of matches in the middle. Shake the box and ask the children in turn, *How many matches are there in the magic matchbox?* |

2 In turn, the children try to guess the number of matches, by asking, *Are there seven? Are there four? Is there only one? Is it empty?* and so on.

3 If a child guesses the correct number, then he or she keeps the matches and becomes the 'teacher' for the next round, taking fresh matches from the pile in the middle.

4 The game continues until all the matches in the middle have been won. The child with the most matches at the end of the game wins.

| **VARIATION 1** | Practise the phrases *How many matches have I got? Have you got …?*, etc. |

VARIATION 2	Instead of matches and a box, use a hat and any objects (marbles, pebbles, pencils, conkers) or flashcards of words which need revising.
COMMENTS	1 If you use matches, it is important that they are spent, to avoid safety problems. Clean the tips of the matches with a wet cloth before playing. 2 When you have demonstrated the game more than one group can play at once.

2.4   Coconut shy

GAME TYPE	**Movement game**
AIMS	**Language:** Revising numbers; simple addition. **Other:** Throwing accurately.
AGE	4+
GROUP SIZE	4–8
TIME	**10–15 minutes**
MATERIALS	Cardboard rolls (kitchen paper or foil rolls are ideal); coloured pens; several soft foam balls; (for Variation 1) a scoreboard.
DESCRIPTION	You can find coconut shies or their equivalent at most fun-fairs. They are usually a set of six tin cans, stacked up in a pyramid, and the idea is to try to knock them down by throwing a ball.
PROCEDURE	1 Give each child a cardboard roll. The children draw funny faces on the cardboard rolls. 2 Stack the rolls into a pyramid on a table at one end of the room. This is the coconut shy. Count the rolls with the children. 3 Put a chair a few feet away from the table. The distance will depend on the size and throwing abilities of the children. In turn, the children throw the ball at the coconut shy from a standing position behind the chair. They try to knock down as many rolls as possible. Count the rolls knocked down and count how many are left.
VARIATION 1	To make the game competitive, introduce a points system. If a child knocks down three cardboard rolls, he or she gets three points, and so on. A child who knocks down all the rolls might be awarded five bonus points. Mark the points on a scoreboard.
VARIATION 2	With larger classes, split the children into teams or have two or three coconut shies set up in various places in the classroom.

COMMENTS

1 Playing this game may become frustrating for a child who keeps missing the coconut shy. Use your discretion and allow weaker children to have more than one attempt or let them stand closer to the target. If the other children find this unfair, allow everyone to have, for example, three throws. You should have three small balls. Otherwise, one of the children stands near the coconut shy and throws the ball back each time.

2 If you have a large class, set up 'game stations' (see the Introduction, page 12) with a different activity in each corner of the classroom. If several groups play 'Coconut shy' at once it could get chaotic.

2.5   Telephone game

GAME TYPE

Role-play game

AIMS

Language: Listening; understanding sequences of numbers; how to answer the phone.
Other: Telephoning skills.

AGE

6+

GROUP SIZE

8–20

TIME

15–20 minutes

MATERIALS

Two identical series of cards with telephone numbers written on them (one card per child); little cardboard telephones for each child or toy telephones; (for Variation 2) situation cards.

DESCRIPTION

The children telephone each other and learn simple telephone language.

PREPARATION

1 Prepare the telephone number cards. Write two numbers, one in red and one in green, on each card. Keep the numbers as distinct as possible for beginners, but make the number series very similar for older or more advanced children. If you are teaching in the children's home country, the phone numbers should correspond to the type of phone numbers they are familiar with, for example six- or seven-digit numbers. You can make sure that all the children will have a turn by making a continuous chain of numbers, with no repetitions.

2 If you have no toy telephones available, you can make cardboard ones using Worksheet 2.5 (see page 137).

PROCEDURE

1 Mix the cards and give one to each child. Explain to the children that the red number is their own telephone number and the green number is the number of one of the other children.

2 Dial the green number on your card, repeating the numbers as you dial. The children listen and look at the red numbers on their cards, to see if it is their number.

3 When a child hears his or her number, he or she picks up a phone and says *Hello, X here*, or the usual answer in your country.

4 The child who answered the teacher's call dials the next number.

5 If a child dials a 'wrong' number, he or she must dial again. Similarly, a number not recognized by any of the other children must be repeated. The game ends when all the children have both dialled and answered the phone. The cards can then be redistributed for a second round.

VARIATION 1

Extend the telephone dialogue into a short conversation. You can either put examples on the board or, in the case of advanced children, leave the conversation to their imagination.

VARIATION 2

Make 10–20 situation cards. Before dialling, child 1 must turn over a situation card, for example, ordering a pizza, inviting someone to a party, or calling directory enquiries to ask for another number. The situations can be directly related to what the children have recently learned or incorporate characters they know, if their coursebook has a running story.

VARIATION 3

Give older children four or five 'green' telephone numbers. When a child dials, he or she may choose any of the numbers.

2.6 Clock race

GAME TYPE

Movement and team game

AIMS

Language: Telling the time; careful listening.
Other: Understanding clocks.

AGE

6+

GROUP SIZE

8–20

TIME

10 minutes

MATERIALS

A set of large numbers (1–12), drawn on pieces of thick A4 paper for each team; a scoreboard.

DESCRIPTION

This is a simple physical response team game. The object is to understand the time and reproduce it by standing on the right numbers of the clock.

PROCEDURE	1 You need a very large classroom or empty space, perhaps the school yard or playground. Lay the numbers on the floor in the form of two clocks, with a wide space between each clock, one clock for each team. The clocks should be approximately the same size. The teams stand or sit at an equal distance away from their clocks.
	2 All together the children ask *What time is it?* Call out a time, for example, *It's seven o'clock.* Two children from each team run to their clocks and stand on the numbers 7 and 12 to show this time. The first team to represent the time correctly gets a point on the scoreboard.
	3 The children go back to their teams and you call out a new time. Two new children from each team run to the clock. The game continues until one team has five or ten points.
VARIATION 1	If a team makes a mistake, say *It isn't seven o'clock. What time is it?* pointing to the time they are representing. The mistaken children say the time they are actually showing on their clock. If they are right, give them half a point.
VARIATION 2	Let the teams say the times to each other. For this variation you could use only one clock, if space is limited.
VARIATION 3	One team shows a time of their choice, and the other team has to tell the time. The child who is the 'long hand' of the clock holds a strip of paper in the air, to avoid confusion.
COMMENTS	Play this game with children who can already tell the time in English. Younger children might only be able to tell full hours, but more advanced children should be able to tell all times. It's possible to play this game even if the children can only tell full hours.

2.7   Goal!

GAME TYPE	**Board and team game**
AIMS	**Language:** Numbers; colours.
AGE	**6+**
GROUP SIZE	**4 (in pairs)**
TIME	**10–15 minutes**
MATERIALS	Game board (see diagram); dice; one counter per group in the shape of a ball or football player; old sports magazines to cut pictures from; (for Variation 1) colour dice; (for Variation 2) picture forfeit cards.

PREPARATION

1 Together with the children make a game board as in the illustration. The board must have 21 spaces.

2 Make a counter in the shape of a ball or football player for each group.

3 Children enjoy decorating the board with a 'football' motif. Provide some old sports magazines for them to cut out pictures. It needn't be football—it can be any other sport with a touch line or a goal.

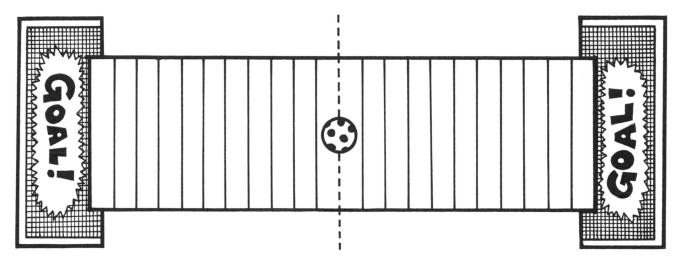

PROCEDURE

1 Place the counter on the space in the middle of the board. A player from Team A rolls the dice and moves in the direction of Team B's goal. The other children chant the number of spaces.

2 A player from team B rolls and moves the game figure in the direction of Team A's goal. Then another player from Team A takes over, and so on.

3 The first team to cross the opponents' line (goal) wins.

VARIATION 1

Add colour spaces and a colour dice. If a child lands on a colour space, he or she must roll the colour dice next turn, moving to the next colour shown on the dice. Some spaces should be half-and-half, giving the children the option of which dice to roll.

VARIATION 2

Add special 'forfeit' spaces. If the children land on these spaces they must draw a card and move forward or backwards according to the pictures on the card.

VARIATION 3

For more advanced groups, the forfeits can be more complex and not directly related to the progress of the game. (For example, *What's your telephone number? When is your birthday?* or something silly like *Walk like an old man.*)

COMMENTS

This relatively easy game works well as a filler for children who finish a task early. It is also helpful for keeping focus if many children trickle into class late.

2.8   Rays of sunlight

GAME TYPE	**Dice game**
AIMS	**Language:** Numbers; revising vocabulary categories; basic game vocabulary. **Other:** Understanding sequences.
AGE	**6+**
GROUP SIZE	**6–10**
TIME	**20–45 minutes (depending on group size and variations)**
MATERIALS	A large sheet of cardboard for each group of 6–10 children; coloured felt tip pens; dice; (for Variation 2) flashcards.
PREPARATION	On the cardboard sheet draw a medium-sized circle with lines coming out from the circle like rays of light. Write the numbers 1–6 on one of the rays of light. Draw as many rays of light as there are children in your group. For large classes draw one per group. Have no more than ten children in each group.

PROCEDURE

1 The children sit in a circle around the sun. Place a dice in the centre of the sun.

2 Explain to the children that the object of the game is to roll the dice and get all the numbers in proper order. Thus, each child must roll first a one, then a two, etc. If a child rolls, for example, a one and then a three, they must pass the dice to the next child, but they can keep the number 1 they rolled. On the next turn, the child must roll a two. Allow each player three rolls of the dice on each turn regardless of the numbers (otherwise the game will take too long).

3 Play a couple of practice rounds to be sure the children understand.

4 The children have to call out their numbers: *I've got a six*, or simply *six* for the very young. You can prompt them during the game by saying *Whose turn is it?* or *Roll the dice*, etc. The winner should call out *Finished*.

VARIATION 1

Numbers are really only symbols for sequences in this game. You can draw a chart with the numbers one to six on the left and any vocabulary you want on the right (colours, animals, etc.). The children roll the dice and try to get the items in the right order, saying, for example, *I've got a cow!*

VARIATION 2

For more advanced children, instead of a sequence they must try to form a grammatical sentence on their ray of light. Place a pile of cards with simple verbs, prepositions, adjectives, and vocabulary items. Children roll the dice and must choose the card corresponding to the number. If a child thinks he or she has a sentence he or she calls out *Ready*. They then say the sentence. The other children must listen and decide if it is correct.

VARIATION 3

For very young children, instead of one large sun with many rays, pair off the children and give each a sun with six rays. The numbers 1–6 correspond to colours. The children roll the dice and colour in the rays. Each ray of the sun must be a separate colour. The first team to colour in all their rays wins.

COMMENTS

Although, with the exception of variation 2, this game requires little active speaking, it is a good way to revise vocabulary and can serve as a basic game structure which you can modify to suit your particular needs.

2.9 Body clocks

GAME TYPE

Movement game

AIMS

Language: *What time is it? It's … .*
Other: Spatial awareness; ability to tell the time.

AGE

8+

GROUP SIZE

4–12

TIME

5–10 minutes

DESCRIPTION

This is a simple miming game. The object is to represent times by using parts of the body.

PROCEDURE

1 The children stand in a circle in a very wide open space, with a few feet between each. They ask *What time is it?*
2 Say a time, for example, *It's three o'clock*. The children now put their arms up to represent this time: right arm straight up and left arm out to the side. If a child makes a mistake, he or she is out.
3 The last child left in wins.
4 Children who are out should continue to be involved. Get them to sit or stand outside the circle and continue miming the times. Alternatively, children who are out say the times and check that the others are miming correctly.

VARIATION 1

Make the game into a competition between two teams, giving each team different times to represent.

VARIATION 2

Instead of using their arms, children pair up and represent the times by lying on the floor inside a huge clock (numbers written in chalk on the floor or flashcards with the numbers 1–12). In this version, make a tall child be the long hand and a shorter child the short hand of the clock.

VARIATION 3

In order to speed up the game, the last child to put his or her arms in the right position is out.

COMMENTS

1 Play this game with children who are able to tell the time in English. Make sure that the children understand that they should represent the times with their arms as the hands of a clock.

2 Make it clear that the clock face should be as seen by opposite players, i.e. not back to front. If this is confusing (with younger children), stick to Variation 2.

3 To increase the visible understanding of this game, give each child a long strip of thick cardboard to hold, representing the long hand of the clock.

2.10 Big clock game

GAME TYPE

Movement or board game

AIMS

Language: Present simple; telling the time.

AGE

7+

GROUP SIZE

6–10

TIME

30–45 minutes

MATERIALS

Eight cardboard clocks with varying times (see Worksheet 2.10 on page 138); about 20 colourful cardboard squares to be spaces for a 'real-life' game board; dice (if available, a very large sponge dice, which can be rolled on the floor and is visible to the whole class); (for Variations) forfeit cards; action picture cards.

PROCEDURE

1 Clear a large space in the classroom. Distribute the cardboard squares and the clocks around the room, making a winding snake. This is the track of the life-sized board game.

2 Child 1 rolls the dice and moves forward.

3 If child 1 lands on a clock, he or she must tell the group what he or she normally does at that time: *At six o'clock I eat dinner.*

4 If the answer is correct, the child moves two spaces forward. If the answer is wrong, the child stays still. In turn, the other children may answer the question. If they give a grammatically correct, plausible answer, they may move forward one space.

5 Child 2 now rolls the dice.

6 The first player to reach 'finish' wins.

VARIATION 1

You can include other forfeits or risk spaces along the game path. Mark these spaces with a star. If children land on a star, they must turn the space card over and do whatever is written on the card, for example, *Move four spaces forward/back. Spell your name. Sing the Hokey Cokey.*

VARIATION 2

Use the present continuous instead of the present simple. In this variation, place a pile of about ten cards by each clock. The cards show pictures of actions familiar to the children. If players land on a clock, they take a card (for example, skiing). They must say what he/she/they are doing at that time, for example *It's three o'clock. They are skiing.*

2.11 Higher or lower?

GAME TYPE

Dice game

AIMS

Language: Revising numbers; *I've got … You've got …* comparatives.
Other: Simple addition; understanding probabilities.

AGE

8+

GROUP SIZE

4–6

TIME

5–10 minutes

MATERIALS

Three dice per group; shaker; scoreboard; (for Variation 2) playing cards or flashcards.

PROCEDURE

1 Demonstrate the game to the whole class before dividing the children into groups of 4–6.

2 Child 1 rolls the three dice and adds up the points, saying, for example *I've got 14.* He or she then passes the dice and shaker to child 2.

3 Child 2 now guesses whether he or she will roll a lower or higher number, saying *Lower!* or *Higher!* and rolling the dice.

4 If child 2 guesses correctly, he or she says, for example *I've got 13! 13 is lower than 14!* and gets a point on the scoreboard. If child 2 guessed incorrectly then another child can say *You've got 17! 17 is higher than 14!* and score a point.

5 Each child takes it in turn to guess whether he or she will roll a number higher or lower than the previously rolled number.

6 After a prearranged number of rounds, add the points up and the child with the most wins.

VARIATION 1

If available, use one 12- or 20-sided number dice, instead of the three standard dice. These are available from some specialist games shops.

VARIATION 2   Instead of dice, use a set of standard playing cards or flashcards with 'strength values'. Practise the structure *My lion's stronger than your tiger!* etc.

2.12 Money in the middle

GAME TYPE   **Dice game**

AIMS   **Language:** *Please give me … Can I have … Would you like …?*
Other: Understanding the difference between left and right.

AGE   **8+**

GROUP SIZE   **4–10**

TIME   **15 minutes**

MATERIALS   One 'star' dice per group (see Worksheet 2.12 on page 139); shaker; toy money; (for Variation 1) toys, beans, counters, small cards, etc.

DESCRIPTION   The object of the game is to be the only player with money.

PREPARATION   Make a 'rules' board large enough for all the children to see (see Procedure, step 2).

PROCEDURE   1 Demonstrate the game to the whole class before dividing the children into groups. Give each child three dollars at the beginning of the game.

2 In turn, the children roll the dice. They must obey the following rules:

If you roll	
1 or 2	give $1 to the player on your left.
3 or 4	give $1 to the player on your right.
5	keep your money.
☆ (star)	put $1 in the middle.

Photocopiable © Oxford University Press

3 If a child rolls 1, 2, 3, or 4, the others say *Would you like a dollar? Please give me a dollar*, etc. Money put in the middle is out of the game.

4 Children with no money left may not roll the dice, but are not out of the game, because they might still receive money from the children sitting next to them. When only one child has any money left, he or she wins the game.

VARIATION 1	Instead of money, use toys, pieces of coloured paper, beans, counters, sweets, or small memory cards on a theme you would like the children to practise.
VARIATION 2	Allow older children to make up new rules. They write them down on a new rules board.
VARIATION 3	Instead of a star dice, use an ordinary dice and put $1 in the middle when a six is thrown.
VARIATION 4	You can of course use whatever currency you like.
COMMENTS	You can make star dice by putting little stickers on the faces of a regular dice and drawing on them. This could influence how the dice roll.

2.13 First to say Z!

AIMS	**Language:** The alphabet or numbers.
AGE	8+
GROUP SIZE	4–12
TIME	5–10 minutes
MATERIALS	A small, soft ball; a scoreboard.
DESCRIPTION	The object of the game is to be the first to say the letter Z . The children should have a firm knowledge of the alphabet.
PROCEDURE	1 The children sit in a circle. The first child holds the ball and starts the first round. A child may say one, two, or maximum three letters of the alphabet before passing the ball to the next child. For example, Child 1 says *ABC*, child 2 says *D*, child 3 says *EFG*, child 4 says *HI*.
	2 The child who says the letter *Z* wins the round and gets a point. He or she then starts a new round. The game continues until a child has three points.
VARIATION 1	Instead of the letters of the alphabet, the children count, saying one, two or three numbers. The child who says the number 20 wins a point. Try this version backwards too, counting down from 20 to zero.
VARIATION 2	Play the game with the months of the year, starting with January. In this version, the children may only say one or two months. The child who says *December* wins a point.

VARIATION 3   Use the technique of this game to read out a story, say a rhyme or chant, sing a song, etc. In each case the child saying the last word wins the round and starts the next one.

3 Colours

Colours are almost as universal as numbers but they are less concrete than you may think. Colours are subjective and working with them sets off a large amount of creative potential among children. Perceptions of colour, and choices of colours in drawings, are highly personal. Colours reflect feelings and moods. In short, colours are a multi-layered topic with high communicative potential.

The games in this chapter are relatively simple and aim at getting the children comfortable with using the English names for colours. We have not included more complex colour games here, since most have other characteristics beyond the colour component. Like numbers, colours can be used with virtually any other theme. Chapter 8, 'Multi-purpose games', and the Variations in other chapters, provide lots of material to expand on the colour theme.

3.1 Colour chain

GAME TYPE	**Card game**
AIMS	**Language:** Colours. **Other:** Distinguishing primary and secondary colours.
AGE	4+
GROUP SIZE	8–20
TIME	**10–15 minutes**
MATERIALS	Three sets of coloured cards; (for Variations) sets of picture flashcards.
PROCEDURE	1 Divide the children into teams. The teams sit in lines with their backs to you, except the first player on each team, who should face you. 2 Give the player at the other end of each line a set of colour flashcards. You also have a set. 3 When everybody is ready, hold up a colour card. The players facing you look at the card and whisper the colour down the line. The last player on each team must choose the correct colour from the set of flashcards and hold it up. If the colour is correct the team gets one point.

4 The last player now goes to the front of the line and faces you. Start again.

5 After 10–15 minutes, the team with the most points wins.

VARIATION 1

You can replace colours with other pictures such as animals or toys, and of course combinations such as *a red balloon*, *a black cat*, etc.

VARIATION 2

For advanced children, you can introduce flashcards with simple scenes such as swimming or eating dinner. Or if your class is very good, you can glue pictures from magazines onto flashcards, for the children to describe.

COMMENTS

In Variation 2 there may not be a 'right' and 'wrong' answer, depending on the pictures on the flashcard, so you may want to do away with points.

3.2 Feed the mouse

GAME TYPE

Movement game

AIMS

Language: Calling out colours.
Other: Catching.

AGE

4–6

GROUP SIZE

4–10

TIME

5 minutes

MATERIALS

Mouse hand puppet; thick paper; coloured pens; scissors.

PREPARATION

With the children prepare small triangles of 'cheese' of various colours, using thick paper, coloured pens, and scissors. The children might need help in cutting out the cheese if they are not used to scissors.

PROCEDURE

1 Show the children the mouse hand puppet, which you keep on your hand throughout the game.

2 Throw the pieces of cheese into the air, one at a time, calling out the colour.

3 The children try to catch the cheese. To avoid a skirmish, only two or three children may try to catch each piece of cheese. A child who has caught a piece of cheese then feeds the mouse, by putting the cheese into its mouth.

VARIATION 1

After two rounds, the children call out the colours of the cheese.

VARIATION 2

Once the children know the colours, they can, in turn, take over the role of teacher and throw the cheese.

VARIATION 3	Throw two or more different coloured pieces of cheese in the air. The children call out the colour of the cheese they catch.
COMMENTS	1 This is a simple but effective game for introducing the colours. However, because of its simplicity it is only useful for very young learners.
	2 The pieces of cheese should be of a size which flies well.
	3 Be aware that cheese is an uncountable noun. If you want to add numbers and counting to this game, try using *a monkey* and *a banana*, for example.

3.3 Target balloon game

GAME TYPE	**Movement game**
AIMS	**Language:** Revising colours. **Other:** Recognizing colours.
AGE	4–6
GROUP SIZE	4–10
TIME	**10 minutes**
MATERIALS	Balloons (various colours); coloured paper in the same colours; a large box; (for Variation) straws.
PREPARATION	Blow up the balloons before the game. Store the balloons in a large box.
PROCEDURE	1 Show the children a balloon, saying *This is a balloon.* Ask the children *What colour's the balloon?*
	2 Give each child a balloon, asking for the colour.
	3 Put the pieces of coloured paper around the room.
	4 The children take their balloons to the piece of paper with the same colour.
VARIATION	Make the game competitive: for example, the children blow the balloons from one end of the room to the coloured paper at the other end, without touching them. Try the same variation but blowing the balloons with straws.

3.4 Mouse race

GAME TYPE	**Board game**
AIMS	**Language:** Revising colours and numbers; game-playing terms. **Other:** Recognizing colours.
AGE	4+
GROUP SIZE	6–12
TIME	**10–15 minutes**
MATERIALS	Large board (see Worksheet 3.4, page 140); coloured pens; paper; scissors; glue; dice.

PREPARATION

1 Before class prepare the game board: one for each team if your class is larger than 12. Draw a mouse cage at one end of the board. This is the start. Draw a large piece of cheese at the other end of the board to represent the finish. For each two players draw one track with at least 40 spaces. All tracks should be the same length. Colour the spaces with two different colours alternately. The board may also be made by the children as a craft activity.

2 The children make small paper mice. Show the children an example of a mouse which they can easily copy. Each child colours his or her mouse in one of the colours on the playing board tracks. There should be two mice of each colour.

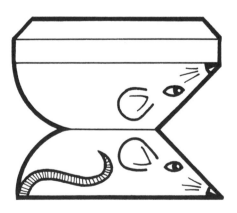 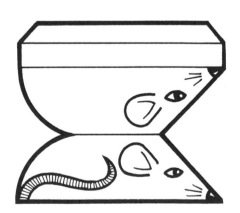

PROCEDURE

1 In turn, the children throw the dice and move their mouse along the track with the same colour as their mouse. As they do so they count aloud and repeat the colour of their mouse, for example, *One, two, three, four—red, red, red, red* or *red one, red two, red three, red four.*

2 The first mouse to reach the cheese wins.

3 Play this game a few times over the course of several lessons, changing each child's colour, so that they practise all the colours.

VARIATION 1

If a child throws a six, his or her mouse gets tired and doesn't move for that go.

VARIATION 2

Add mouse-traps to the board at various intervals. If a mouse lands on a mouse-trap it misses the next turn.

COMMENTS

This is an excellent simple board game, which can be used for teaching all kinds of game-playing terms, for example, *Please give me the dice, It's my/your turn, Miss a turn.*

3.5 Colour dodge

GAME TYPE

Movement game

AIMS

Language: *I'm on …* (+ colours); questions and answers (Variation 2).
Other: Quick recognition and reactions.

AGE

4+

GROUP SIZE

8–30

TIME

10–15 minutes

MATERIALS

A large number of cardboard squares of at least six different colours; Blu-tack; a bell or buzzer; music (optional); (for Variation 1) flashcards.

PREPARATION

You need a large open space to play this game. With Blu-tack or sticky tape stick down a large number of coloured cardboard squares, at least as many as there are children, around the playing area. Make sure there are no tables, chairs, or other objects with sharp corners nearby.

PROCEDURE

1 Shout *Go!* and the children start hopping around the room or dancing to music.

2 Ring the bell and shout out a colour, for example, *Blue!*

3 The children now have to hop onto a coloured card—any colour except the one you called out. Ring the bell a second time. Once the children have 'landed' on a coloured card, they must stop. Only one child may stand on each card.

4 Now the children, in turn, call out quickly where they are, for example, *I'm on red!* (for very young children, *Red!* is enough). Children who don't manage to reach a card before you ring the bell a second time are 'nowhere'.

5 All the children who are either on the colour you called or 'nowhere' are out. Quickly take away the same number of cards as children who are out.

6 Continue playing until there is only one child left. This child then takes over the role of teacher and a new game begins. Make sure the pace of this game is always fast, so that the children who are 'out' don't get bored.

VARIATION 1

If you have enough flashcards on different themes, you can use this game to revise vocabulary.

VARIATION 2

With older children, give the children who are on the 'wrong' colour card or 'nowhere' the chance to stay in the game if they answer a question correctly. In this way, you can revise phrases from any area of the curriculum.

3.6   Colour blindfold

GAME TYPE	**Movement and guessing game**
AIMS	**Language:** *What colour is …?* Colours; clothing; simple possessives. **Other:** Memory.
AGE	6+
GROUP SIZE	6–12
TIME	**10–15 minutes**
MATERIALS	A blindfold.

PROCEDURE

1 Make a circle with the children. Ask them a few questions about their clothing or yours, such as *What colour is Nina's shirt?* or *What colour are Robert's socks?*

2 Show the children the blindfold. Choose one child, preferably a confident one, to come to the centre of the circle. Blindfold him or her.

3 The children in the circle ask questions using the phrase *What colour is X's …?* If the child in the middle guesses correctly, he or she removes the blindfold and gives it to the child whose clothing colour was correctly guessed. Guide the children's questions so that they don't ask only about one or two children's clothes.

4 Once the children have played a few rounds and are comfortable with the game, you can blindfold yourself. Now the children must ask you questions.

VARIATION 1

Instead of using the phrase *What colour is …?* the children ask questions such as *Is Tina's jumper blue?*

VARIATION 2

Instead of the children asking the blindfolded child questions, have him or her make statements such as *Tina's shoes are yellow*, which the children in the circle must answer with *Yes* or *No* (or *True* or *False* for the older children). The child in the middle passes on the blindfold when he or she has made a true statement.

VARIATION 3

Ask *What's Tom wearing?* This changes the focus to clothing.

COMMENTS

1 For the youngest children it may be necessary for you to ask the questions or prompt the children by whispering to them.

2 In step 4, tie the blindfold so that you can see what the children are doing. Most scarves and similar fabrics are see-through if you don't fold them enough times. Make sure the children can't see though!

4 Body parts and clothes

Moving from the large universal topics of numbers and colours, we return to more specific, concrete themes. Games in this chapter tend to be 'rousing' with a lot of movement and general excitement. See Chapter 10, 'Old favourites', and the Index, for some more examples. Body parts and clothes are also very visual subjects and many of the activities can be linked with art and craft activities.

Clothes and body parts should be treated with special care. Be sure that games with clothes do not embarrass children who may have little money or have to wear clothes which are not 'in'. Also bear in mind that children could have disabilities, including missing limbs, especially in war zones, which could make body parts games potentially very upsetting.

The key language function in this chapter is describing. New language items include *He/She's wearing*, adjectives, and of course the vocabulary itself.

4.1 Body fishing

GAME TYPE	**Movement and drawing game**
AIMS	**Language:** Learning body parts. **Other:** Drawing.
AGE	4+
GROUP SIZE	4–8
TIME	**5 minutes**
MATERIALS	Paper; coloured pens; scissors; straws; (for Variation 4) a large sheet of paper.
PREPARATION	The children draw pictures of people and cut them up into individual body parts (hands, legs, feet, hair, nose, etc.). For young children provide outlines of the body and if necessary help cut up the pictures. Make sure each individual body part is clearly recognizable. If not, you can quickly draw more details on them.
PROCEDURE	1 Spread out the body parts randomly in a large circle.
	2 Give each child a straw. Call out the name of a body part. The children look for it and try to suck it up with their straws.
	3 When all body parts are gone from the circle the child with the most wins.

VARIATION 1	Each child has to try to 'reconstruct' a whole person.
VARIATION 2	You can substitute monsters for pictures of people. These monsters can have three noses, six eyes, etc.
VARIATION 3	Once the children know the names of the body parts, they can do the calling.
VARIATION 4	Play as a team game. One child from each team sucks up the required body part and brings it to his or her team. The other team members then stick the body part to a poster.

4.2 Face dice

GAME TYPE	**Dice game**
AIMS	**Language:** Face and/or body vocabulary; basic game language. **Other:** Recognizing written numbers; drawing; matching.
AGE	**5+**
GROUP SIZE	**6–10**
TIME	**15 minutes**
MATERIALS	Dice; paper and pens for drawing; blackboard.
PREPARATION	Write the numbers 1–6 on the left of the blackboard. Draw an arrow from each number to a picture on the right-hand side. Each picture should be a part of a face, for example, *nose*, *mouth*, *eye*, *ear*, *tongue*, or *eyebrows*.
PROCEDURE	1 Give each child a piece of paper and put some pens in the middle. 2 Explain to the children that they need to draw a face with all the face parts on the board. Demonstrate by rolling the dice and pointing, and show that each face part has a corresponding number. 3 Child 1 rolls the dice. He or she must call out the number and the corresponding body part. 4 Child 1 passes the dice to the child on the left and draws the face part he or she rolled. The next child does the same, and so on. 5 If a child rolls a number he or she has already rolled, the dice moves on to the next player. 6 The first child to complete a full face wins.
VARIATION 1	You can replace face parts with body parts or parts of animals, vehicles, etc.

VARIATION 2 Instead of simply repeating numbers and face parts, make the children say phrases when they roll the dice. For example, the group could chant *What did you roll?* and the child responds *I rolled a 2.* The group could then chant *What's a two?* The child responds *2 is a mouth.*

VARIATION 3 For older children, you can use two dice (numbers 2–12) and eleven different face or body parts. Be aware, however, that the chances of rolling 2 or 12 with two dice are small. Instead of allocating a face part to these numbers, let them function as 'joker' numbers. If a child rolls 2 or 12, he or she may choose any face part which he or she hasn't already drawn.

COMMENTS This game is aimed at passive understanding with young children. It is important to talk to the children during the game and get them to understand the words they are saying in different contexts. If you opt for Variation 2 practise the phrases before introducing them into the game. Don't worry about accuracy with these phrases. The children will use them as 'chunks' at first and only with time will they give meaning to all the words.

4.3 Look closely

GAME TYPE **Guessing game**

AIMS **Language:** *What's different? He/She's wearing …*; clothing and other accessories.
Other: Observation.

AGE 6+

GROUP SIZE **6–15**

TIME **10–15 minutes**

MATERIALS Clothing (trousers, shirts, hats, glasses, etc.).

PROCEDURE
1 Place a box with all the clothing in the centre of the classroom. The children stand in a circle around it.
2 Choose one child to come to the box. Explain that this child will choose three new pieces of clothing. Pick up clothing to demonstrate as you explain.
3 Motion the children in the circle to turn their backs to the box. Tell them to shut their eyes.
4 The child in the centre chooses three pieces of clothing and puts them on. The new clothes can be placed discreetly but may not be hidden.

5 The player in the middle asks *What's different?*

6 The children in the circle must answer *He/She's wearing …*

VARIATION 1	Turn the game into a team game. One team dresses up one of its players, while the other team guesses. For each correct guess, the team receives two points, but each wrong guess loses one point. Each player may ask only one question per round. Limit the time the team has for guessing.
VARIATION 2	If you have enough dressing-up clothes, divide the class into two teams and line them up facing each other. In this variation, each player from Team A puts on two extra pieces of clothing. Team B must guess what is different.
VARIATION 3	You can dress up. Let the children guess. This is a good option for the younger children.
VARIATION 4	Replace *He/She's wearing …* with *He/She's got … on.*
COMMENTS	You may want to play this game with the children in a line, since in a circle it can be difficult to see who is peeking.

4.4 Monster waltz

GAME TYPE	**Drawing game**
AIMS	**Language:** Describing pictures. **Other:** Fast drawing; imagination.
AGE	6+
GROUP SIZE	6–12
TIME	**10–15 minutes**
MATERIALS	Four large pieces of paper (such as A3) for each group; coloured pens; music.
DESCRIPTION	The object of the game is to draw crazy monsters and then describe them, using simple phrases, combining body parts with colours, adjectives, etc.
PROCEDURE	1 Put the four large sheets of paper on the four sides of a long rectangular table and the pens in the middle. Turn on the music. 2 The children dance around the table. Stop the music at random. Each child takes a coloured pen and starts drawing one body part of a monster on the nearest sheet of paper. Allow only a few seconds for this, then start the music again.

During each pause in the music, the children may only draw one body part on one of the sheets of paper. There is only one monster per sheet of paper, but it can have many body parts, for example three eyes, four ears, or seven arms. The game continues until you consider the monsters are finished.

3 Hold up each of the finished monsters and let the children describe them. Younger children might simply count the body parts and say *three eyes* or the colours of the body parts. More advanced children should use as many different phrases as possible, for example, *This monster has three eyes*, or *That monster has wings. It can fly.*

VARIATION

When the music stops, say which body parts the children should draw, for example, *Draw eyes!* The children draw as many eyes as possible until the music starts again.

FOLLOW-UP

Give the monsters names and let the children think up stories about them, or describe details such as hobbies, families, personalities, or favourite foods.

4.5 Wacky art competition

GAME TYPE

Drawing game

AIMS

Language: Imperatives; describing pictures.
Other: Drawing; imagination.

AGE

6+

GROUP SIZE

4–12

TIME

10–15 minutes

MATERIALS

Large paper (for example, A3); coloured pens.

DESCRIPTION

This is a kind of drawing dictation game with a difference. You not only dictate what the children are supposed to draw, but also how they should do it!

PROCEDURE

1 The children sit on the floor in a large circle. Each child has a large piece of paper. Put the coloured pens in the middle.

2 In the first round you should do the dictating. Demonstrate the actions, so that the children know what to do. From the second round onwards, the children can, in turn, take over the role of teacher. Here are some ideas for wacky dictations; you and the children can expand upon them, as far as your imaginations go.

- draw with a pen between your feet
- draw with a pen in your mouth
- draw with your left hand (for left-handers with your right hand)

– draw with a pen between your elbows
– draw behind your back without looking

What the children draw (and with which colours) can also be part of the dictation.

3 When the pictures are finished, the children describe them, using all the phrases they know.

FOLLOW-UP

Get the children to guess what each other's drawings are. More advanced children could write what their pictures are supposed to be on the back. In turn, the children try to guess the pictures and receive one point for each correct guess.

4.6 Dressing-up relay

GAME TYPE

Team and movement game

AIMS

Language: *I'm wearing … He's/She's wearing … .*
Other: Fast dressing and undressing (co-ordination).

AGE

6+

GROUP SIZE

8–30

TIME

10–15 minutes

MATERIALS

An identical set of clothes for each team.

DESCRIPTION

This is a team game. The object of the game is for each child to put on one article of clothing, say what it is, then take it off again, passing it to the next child in the team as quickly as possible. It is a relay race.

PROCEDURE

1 Split the class into two or more teams. The teams sit at one end of the room. At the other end of the room put the clothes in separate heaps for each team. Start the relay race by saying *Put on your socks!* The first child from each team runs to the pile of clothes, searches for the socks and puts them on. He or she then runs back to the team, says *I'm wearing socks!* and takes them off again, passing the socks to the second child, who puts them on.

2 The second child runs to the pile of clothes, chooses any article, puts it on and runs back to the team. The child says, for example, *I'm wearing socks and shoes!* He or she then takes both articles of clothing off and passes them to the next child.

3 The game continues in this way until one team has put all the clothes on. The first team to do this wins. One team member will be fully dressed at the end of the game. Referee this relay race very strictly, making sure the children continue using the phrases for each piece of clothing.

VARIATION 1	Instead of taking the clothes off again, the children keep them on. The next player then says *I'm wearing shoes and she's wearing socks!*
VARIATION 2	Let the teams tell each other what the next piece of clothing should be.
VARIATION 3	After playing this game once, try it in reverse. The child who is fully dressed gets undressed, item by item, and passes each article of clothing to another team member, who puts it on. This is a useful variation for practising *I'm (not) wearing …*

4.7   Seasons quartet

GAME TYPE	**Card game**
AIMS	**Language:** Seasons; clothing; *Have you got …?* or *Do you have…?*
AGE	7+
GROUP SIZE	4–8
TIME	**20–30 minutes**
MATERIALS	Firm cardboard cards the size of playing cards with pictures of clothes that are worn in different seasons. You need at least four per season, and one set per group.
DESCRIPTION	The object of the game is for the children to collect all the clothing for a particular season.
PROCEDURE	1 Divide the class into groups of 4–8.
	2 Mix the cards and deal them out to the children. The children can play individually or in teams of two.
	3 The children sort their cards.
	4 Child 1 chooses another child and asks *Have you got something for (winter)?*
	5 If the child does have something for this season he or she answers *Yes, I've got a (scarf)* and gives that card to child 1.
	6 Child 1 puts one card in the middle.
	7 The next child can either take the card from the middle or ask for a card from another child. He or she must also put a card down—everyone thus keeps the same number of cards.
	8 The first child to collect all the clothes for a particular season wins.
VARIATION 1	Add plurals and singulars. The children must collect either all plurals, for example, *shoes, socks, gloves,* or all singulars, for example, *shirt, jacket, raincoat.*

VARIATION 2

Add colours. The children must collect all the clothing of one colour. They must ask for *blue socks* or *a red jumper*, etc.

COMMENTS

Be aware that not all clothes are worn in just one season, especially Autumn and Spring clothes. Choose the clothes very carefully or allow discussion.

4.8 Who is the boss?

GAME TYPE

Movement and guessing game

AIMS

Language: Present continuous.
Other: Quick reactions; observation.

AGE

8+

GROUP SIZE

8–25

TIME

15–20 minutes

PROCEDURE

1 The object of the game is to find out who is the boss. Explain to the children that the 'boss' is someone who is in charge, a leader or captain, for example. Explain that a commentator is someone who tells radio or television listeners what is happening at a sporting event, and that a detective is a person who finds criminals.

2 The children choose a detective, who leaves the room. The rest of the children (quietly) choose a 'boss' and a commentator.

3 The children sit in a circle, all doing the same action (for example, clapping hands or snapping fingers). Ask the detective to come back into the room.

4 The commentator says *We're clapping hands*. The children continue to do this action but secretly watch the 'boss'. When the boss changes the action, all the players must try to do the same action almost immediately, so that the detective will not see who the boss is.

5 The commentator always describes each new action. If the detective believes he or she knows who the boss is, he or she says *Stop! I think the boss is …* . If the guess is right, the detective joins the other children and the commentator becomes the new detective, leaving the room for a new round. If a detective guesses wrongly, he or she must watch more closely. If the child guesses wrongly three times, he or she must do a forfeit, for example, sing a song.

6 The game is over when the fun begins to diminish or when all the children have been either detective, commentator, or boss.

4.9 Magazine flip

GAME TYPE	**Team game**
AIMS	**Language:** Describing people; present participles. **Other:** Quick recognition.
AGE	**8+**
GROUP SIZE	**4–12**
TIME	**10–15 minutes**
MATERIALS	A large selection of colourful magazines and/or catalogues with lots of pictures of people.
PROCEDURE	1 Split the class into teams. Give each team an equal number of magazines. There should be more magazines than children. 2 Tell the teams what to look for, for example, *Find a man wearing a blue hat*, or *Look for a woman riding a bicycle*. The children quickly flip through their magazines and try to find a picture that resembles what you said. The first team to do so shouts *Stop!* The team shows the picture and gets a point if it is correct. The first team to get five points wins.
VARIATION 1	After two rounds, the teams have to swap three magazines. This limits any bias that might occur from the differences between the magazines.
VARIATION 2	The child who finds the right picture dictates the next picture, so that the children practise saying the phrases.
VARIATION 3	When a picture has been found, the team can get extra points for describing other aspects of the person in the picture.
VARIATION 4	Apart from people, you can describe anything that is often in magazines, for example houses, furniture, animals, vehicles, etc. Advertisement leaflets are also useful as identical sets can be given to the teams.
COMMENTS	1 This is a simple recognition game, which is fun and also useful for practising many different phrases. 2 Before class check the magazines to ensure that they contain pictures on the subjects of your choice and that they are suitable for children.

4.10 Fashion show

GAME TYPE	**Role-play game**
AIMS	**Language:** *He's/She's wearing…*; describing people and clothes. **Other:** Imagination.
AGE	8+
GROUP SIZE	6–12
TIME	**45–60 minutes**
MATERIALS	Clothes; make-up; music; fake microphone; a set of six large cards with numbers 1–6 for each child; red carpet (optional).
DESCRIPTION	This is a team game, with two children in each team. The children play the roles of model and commentator in a pretend fashion show.
PROCEDURE	**Lesson 1**

Lesson 1

1 Explain to the children what a fashion show is, how it works, and what models and commentators do.

2 Put the children into pairs and tell them that they are going to put on a fashion show. Show them the clothes. They plan what they want to wear—the props that can be used are almost unlimited. They might need to bring extra clothes and props from home.

3 The pairs prepare the commentary, describing the clothes and models. The children should use as much language as they know. Help them to include a few new words or phrases.

Lesson 2

1 The children dress up, put on make-up, play background music, etc. Give each child a set of six cards, numbered 1–6.

2 In turn, each pair gives its fashion show presentation. The other children sit in two long lines opposite each other. If available, lay out a long piece of (red) carpet in the middle for the models to walk up and down. One member of the team is the 'model' and walks between the lines of children, showing off the beautiful clothes.

3 Using a fake microphone, the other member of the team commentates, for example: *Here we can see Gina. She's a young model, only nine years old. She's got long brown hair and a happy smile. She's wearing black stockings, a red blouse and a white skirt.* Set a time limit for each presentation, so that the spectators do not get bored.

4 After each presentation, the other children give marks for the model, by holding up a card from 1 to 6. Once a mark has been given, the card is taken out of the game. This avoids cheating by giving the lowest mark all the time. Every player should be model

and commentator at least once. The model with the highest marks wins.

COMMENTS

The technique of taking the marks cards out when they have been used once is absolutely vital to the success of the fashion show as a game. The children only give marks to the opposing teams, thus increasing the tactical use of the marks cards and adding an enormous amount of tension and excitement to the fashion show.

5 Animals

Animals fascinate children. They come in all shapes, colours, and sizes. Animals can fly, swim, run, hop, or just wiggle. Some are fast and others barely move at all. They live all over the world— in nests, holes, or dens, sometimes alone and sometimes in groups. Some animals are pets and live with people. Many children have pets which they love very much. The animal kingdom is so diverse that there is no end to the projects you can devise with them.

But animals also have characteristics. We attribute certain traits to different types of animals. Snakes are sly in English-speaking culture. Lions are courageous and just. Monkeys are fun and mischievous. Owls are wise. In other cultures animals may have different attributes. Animals are close enough to humans to become characters in their own right. Animals are great for setting up role plays and they give children a mask to hide behind if they are shy.

The games in this chapter focus on identifying individual animals and discovering their characteristics (big, small, loud, etc.) and abilities (can they swim, jump, fly, etc.?), and making comparisons, for example, *A lion is big, but an elephant is bigger.*

5.1 Now you're on my side

GAME TYPE	**Team and guessing game**
AIMS	**Language:** *Are you …? Yes, I am/No, I'm not.*
AGE	4+
GROUP SIZE	10–20
TIME	**10–15 minutes** (Larger groups may take longer.)
MATERIALS	Small cards with pictures of animals, or written names for older groups. You need at least one card per child, but they do not all have to be different; (for Variation) pictures of famous people.
PREPARATION	In a previous lesson, introduce the animals. The children can help to glue pictures from magazines on to the cards. You can also photocopy outlines for the children to colour in. Do not ask younger children to draw an animal themselves since you will probably not recognize it.
PROCEDURE	1 Put one of each type of animal (picture or word) on the board so that the children can refer to them.

2 Mix the cards. Each child takes a card. Be sure to tell the children not to show their card to the others.

3 Divide the class into two teams. The teams should face each other in two lines. (If the class is very large, make two sets of two teams.)

4 A child from Team A starts. This child approaches any child from Team B and asks *Are you ...?* The player from Team B looks at his or her card and says *Yes, I am* or *No, I'm not.* If the player says *Yes*, he or she must cross over to the other team. Team A can ask further questions until Team B says *No*.

5 When child B says *No*, his or her team asks the next question. Team B may not ask for the animal name of the player they lost until they have correctly guessed another card. The team which brings all the opposing players to their side wins.

VARIATION

For older children replace animals with famous people: pop or film stars, sports figures, television or story characters. If the children cannot think of enough by themselves, add some which you are sure they know. Put up the names, or pictures, if available, for all the children to see.

COMMENTS

The children should take turns to ask the questions, even if the answer is *Yes*. In larger groups this guarantees that everyone gets a chance to speak and the time between turns is not so long as to lead to boredom.

5.2 Jungle race

GAME TYPE

Board game

AIMS

Language: *Can/Can't* + abilities.
Other: Drawing; creativity.

AGE

5+

GROUP SIZE

5–8

TIME

30–45 minutes

MATERIALS

A large playing board (such as A2) and 6–7 small animal picture cards per group (see the flashcards on pages 143–4); counters; dice.

DESCRIPTION

The object of the game is to move from start to finish along the track through the jungle, crossing obstacles with the help of animals.

PREPARATION

Make and decorate the board (and cards, if necessary) with the children in a preceding lesson. You need one board and set of cards for each group of 5–8 children. Draw trees and plants, rivers, streams, mountains, caves, etc. Along the track, draw six or seven 'obstacles' (for example a river, ravine, or snake-pit). See the illustration for an example.

PROCEDURE

1 Put one small animal picture card next to each obstacle. In each case, the animal should have the ability to get past the obstacle (for example, if it's a river, use a card of a big fish or a friendly hippo; if it's a ravine, use a card with an eagle or flamingo). In turn, the children roll the dice and move their counters along the track. When a child reaches an obstacle, he or she must stop and wait. When it is the child's next turn, he or she says, for example, *Here is a ravine.* Ask the child *Can you fly?* The child replies, *No I can't, but the eagle can fly.* The child then puts his or her counter on the eagle card, which flies over the obstacle. The eagle then flies back to its original position, to help any other children over the ravine.

2 The children move their counters around the jungle in this way. The first child to reach the finish wins.

VARIATION 1

Allow extra spaces for the obstacles. When, for example, a child flies by eagle over the ravine, he or she has to roll the dice and move the eagle (with the counter on it) accordingly. If the obstacle is seven spaces long, other children might have to wait until the eagle returns, as it takes at least two rolls of the dice to cross the obstacle. The eagle should return straight away to avoid too much waiting.

VARIATION 2

You could also have two or three different animal cards, all of which can take a child across, placed next to an obstacle.

VARIATION 3

Put small piles of animal cards face down next to each obstacle. Not all of these animals can cross the obstacle. In this case, the child draws a card and says, for example, *This is a monkey. Can a monkey swim (across the river)?* The other children say *Yes, it can*, or *No, it can't.* Allow some discussion to take place, if necessary.

VARIATION 4

Split each group into two. Half of the children move from start to finish, the other half from finish to start. Put animal cards on both sides of an obstacle. This version increases the suspense as it's more difficult to see who is winning. It is also an ideal combination with Variation 1 as it limits the time spent waiting at the obstacles.

VARIATION 5

Make short-cuts and 'long-cuts' along the track. Short-cuts might appear to have fewer spaces, but could have more obstacles to cross.

5.3 Animal noises

GAME TYPE

Role-play and guessing game

AIMS

Language: Animal names; *Am I …? Yes, you are/No, you're not*; *I'm … .*
Other: Sound imitation; miming.

AGE

6–10

GROUP SIZE	**6–12**
TIME	**10 minutes**
MATERIALS	Post-it stickers (or paper with sticky tape or safety pins) with pictures or written names of animals (one per child); (for Variation 1) names of vehicles or other sound-making objects.
PREPARATION	Prepare post-it stickers with pictures or the written names of animals. The children should already know many animals and their English sounds. The children can also draw their own animals.

PROCEDURE

1 The children stand in a line, side by side. Go along the back of the line, sticking one post-it sticker on to the back of each child.

2 Bring the children to the front and show them how to ask each other questions such as *Am I a …?* but instead of saying the name of the animal, they imitate the sound that this animal makes. They may also mime. The child being asked checks the back of the other child, and answers *Yes, you are!* or *No, you're not!* The children mingle and try to find out which animal they are.

3 Monitor to make sure everyone is either asking or being asked. If necessary, pair off the children and change the pairs after about a minute. As soon as children have found out their animal, they run to you and say *I'm a (horse)!* this time using the word for their animal. Check the children's backs. If they are right, they take the post-it sticker off their back, stick it on their front and then go to help the other children who are still playing. If they are wrong, the game simply continues. The game finishes when everyone has found out their animals.

4 Use the same post-it stickers for a second round. Stick them on different children's backs. After two rounds include some new animals.

VARIATION 1

This game also works with vehicles or using any sound-making objects the children know.

VARIATION 2

Instead of using sound imitation, reduce the game to simple mime. Any topic is suitable, for example, classroom objects. The children ask *Have I got a …?* and try to describe the object using mime, for example by pretending to use the object. The answer is either *Yes, you have* or *No, you haven't.*

COMMENTS

Remember that animals make different noises in different languages! For example, a cock says *kikeriki* in German, *coquelicot* or *cocorico* in French, and *cock-a-doodle-doo* in English.

5.4   Fast, freaky animals

GAME TYPE	**Drawing game**
AIMS	**Language:** *Is it a … ? Yes, it is/No, it isn't.* **Other:** Fast drawing.
AGE	**6+**
GROUP SIZE	**4–12**
TIME	**10 minutes**
MATERIALS	Paper and coloured pens or pencils; a small picture card of an animal for each child—see the flashcards on pages 143–4 (for older children, just the written words).
PROCEDURE	1 The object of the game is to draw an animal as quickly as possible, but so that it can be recognized by the other children.
	2 Give each child a piece of paper. Put the pens in the middle.
	3 Deal a small flashcard face down to each child. On the word *Go!* the children look at their flashcards, being careful not to show them to the other children. They then have 15 (or 30) seconds to draw a picture of this animal on the paper.
	4 When the time is up, call *Stop!* and all pens must go back to the middle immediately.
	5 In turn, the children now try to guess what the pictures of these animals are, by asking, for example, *Is it a …?* or *Does your picture show a …?* The child who drew the picture answers. A child who guesses correctly gets two points and the player who drew the picture gets one point.
	6 If a picture is completely unrecognizable, the artist gets no points.
COMMENTS	Awarding points might give better artists an advantage, although the speed factor should even this out a bit.

5.5   Animal posters

GAME TYPE	**Guessing game**
AIMS	**Language:** *Is it …? It feels like a/an …*; directions; possessives. **Other:** Drawing; recognition.
AGE	**6+**
GROUP SIZE	**8–20**
TIME	**15–20 minutes**

MATERIALS

Two large sheets of white cardboard (such as A1); smaller cardboard sheets in a variety of colours; coloured pens or pencils; scissors; Blu-tack or sticky tape for sticking paper to paper; a box or feely bag.

PREPARATION

Before the lesson, draw the torsos of two animals, one on each large sheet of white cardboard. The two animals chosen should be very different from each other: for example, a bird and an elephant, not a cat and a lion. Leave out key body parts such as tails, wings, trunks, horns. Hang the posters on the wall at least one metre apart. Clear some space in front of the wall.

PROCEDURE

Lesson 1

Give out the coloured cardboard. Tell the children to draw and cut out parts of animals. (Tell them which ones.) You may want to give young children especially pre-cut outlines, so that they only need to colour them in. There should be two identical sets of animal parts, one per team.

Lesson 2

1 Divide the class into two teams (or two sets of two teams for very large classes). Each team lines up in front of one of the animal torsos on the wall.

2 Give each team a box or feely bag. In this box are the animal parts the children made in an earlier lesson.

3 Blindfold the first player. This child reaches into the box and takes one animal part. The children then ask *What is it?* Child 1 feels the animal part and answers *It feels like … (a bird's wing, an elephant's trunk, a rhino's horn*, etc.) The child must guess not only the part, but also the correct animal.

4 If the animal part does not match the team's animal torso, blindfold the next child, who takes another animal part.

5 If the team believes the animal part matches their animal torso, the rest of the team guides the blindfolded child to the picture and directs him or her where to place the part. Use words such as *left, right, forward, backwards, up, down, stop, a little more*. Let the children call the instructions all at once—this increases the fun. Make sure that the instructions are in English.

6 After fixing the part to the picture, child 1 takes off the blindfold and returns to the team, giving the blindfold to the next child in line.

7 The team that completes its animal poster first wins.

VARIATION 1

Instead of animal torsos, draw landscapes on the big white sheets. Each landscape should have features clearly identifiable as possible animal habitats (for example, caves for bats, rivers for fish, stables for horses, pens for pigs). Instead of animal parts, use full animal cut-outs. The children have to stick them in the proper habitats.

VARIATION 2	With small classes play the game with one team. The blindfolded child must be guided to the correct picture.
VARIATION 3	For the youngest children play as in Variation 2 but remove the blindfold. The child with the animal part must choose which picture to go to and where to put the part. Once the part has been stuck on, ask the group *Is that right?* The children answer *Yes* or *No.* Choose another child to put the part in the correct place if the first child got it wrong.
VARIATION 4	With older children, include *Where does it go?* if the part is placed incorrectly. Choose another child to put it in the right place. This child must say, for example, *The trunk goes on the elephant* or with Variation 1, *The pig goes in the pen*, or simply *The pig goes here/there.*
COMMENTS	1 If the group is small enough talk to the children about animals during the game. Show them pictures in books. Talk about the sounds they make and what they do. Be flexible and allow discussion.
	2 If you have a felt board, you can cut the parts out of coloured felt, which will stick to the board without any need for tape or Blu-tack.

5.6 Animal checkers

GAME TYPE	**Board game**
AIMS	**Language:** Revision of action verbs; animal names; present continuous or present perfect. **Other:** Decision making; strategic thinking.
AGE	**8+**
GROUP SIZE	**4–8**
TIME	**10 minutes**
MATERIALS	A large checkers board (see the example on page 75) and two identical sets of small animal cards for each group (see the flashcards on pages 143–4).
PROCEDURE	1 Play this game the same way as ordinary checkers, a game which most children will know. If not, play the standard version before trying this one. As with traditional checkers, all cards are equal— no animal is stronger than another.
	2 The object of the game is to capture all of the opposing team's cards. Divide the class into an equal number of teams. Place the two sets of cards on the large checkers board, as in standard checkers.

3 Each team, in turn, moves their cards as in checkers. When a child wants to capture a card from the opposing team, he or she describes what is actually happening, for example, *My eagle is flying over your crocodile. My kangaroo's jumping over your snake.* The children should already have a good knowledge of action verbs and the present continuous. Alternatively, for more advanced children, practise using the present perfect, for example, *My kangaroo has just jumped over your snake.*

4 The first team to capture all the other team's cards wins.

VARIATION

Instead of using the present continuous or present perfect, this game is also ideal for practising comparative forms, for example, *My tiger's faster than your mouse. My elephant's bigger than your cat.*

COMMENTS

This is a language teaching variation of a standard board game. Other board games can be adapted for language teaching, if the children already know the rules. Chess, for example, which is far more complicated than checkers, could be adapted in a similar way. See Chapter 9 for more adaptations of traditional games.

6 Food

Food plays a central role in children's daily routine. They have a very clear idea of what they like and dislike: not only what they eat, but when. Chocolate cookies for breakfast? Cornflakes for dinner? In addition, there is the whole issue of how people eat: fork, knife, spoon? Chopsticks, with your fingers, in a banana leaf? Where a child eats also plays a role: in a restaurant, on a table, on the floor, or in a car.

Food is an excellent theme for multi-cultural classes. Nowhere are cultural and regional variations as readily visible to children as in the area of food. Food is probably one of the first contacts a child will make with a foreign culture.

Games in this chapter concentrate on expressing likes and dislikes, classifying food, and polite requests (as in a restaurant).

6.1 Fruit and prepositions relay

GAME TYPE	**Movement and team game**
AIMS	**Language:** Prepositions (*in*, *on*, *under*, *over*).
AGE	**4+**
GROUP SIZE	**8–16**
TIME	**15–30 minutes**
MATERIALS	Two identical sets of familiar fruits, for example, apples, oranges, pears, bananas, peaches; a whistle.
PROCEDURE	

1 Clear a space in the classroom and divide the children into two teams. They stand in lines at one end of the room. At the other end of the room set up two tables facing the two teams. Place the fruit on the tables.

2 Stand between the first two children and say, for example, *Put the apple on a chair*, or *Put the banana under the table*. Blow the whistle to start.

3 The children run to the other end of the room, carry out your instructions, and run back to their lines. The first child to get back to the line earns a point for his or her team.

4 If a child chooses the wrong fruit or puts it in the wrong place, the team gets no points.

5 Play one or two rounds and add up the points.

| VARIATION 1 | Make the game more difficult by calling out more complicated tasks, for example: *Put the apple in the bookshelf and the pear under the teacher's desk,* or *Give the teacher a banana and put a peach next to the door.* |

VARIATION 1

Make the game more difficult by calling out more complicated tasks, for example: *Put the apple in the bookshelf and the pear under the teacher's desk,* or *Give the teacher a banana and put a peach next to the door.*

VARIATION 2

Instead of putting the fruit on a table, tell the children to get an object from anywhere in the room, for example, *Get a book. Find a pencil.* You can also use Variation 1 with *Put* and *Give.*

COMMENTS

If you have uneven numbers or a reluctant child, he or she could call out the commands. With younger children you will need to prompt them by whispering to them or repeating the command after them so that the others understand.

6.2 The *Do you like ...?* game

GAME TYPE

Board game

AIMS

Language: *Do you like ...? Yes, I do/No, I don't. Can you ...? Yes, I can/No, I can't* (Variation 1).
Other: Counting.

AGE

4+ (7+ for Variations 3 and 4)

GROUP SIZE

6–10

TIME

20–30 minutes

MATERIALS

One game board for each group with counters and dice; 7–8 cards with pictures of food; 50 red and 50 blue cards; marker pen; (for variations) cards with pictures of actions, body parts, etc.

PREPARATION

Make a simple game board (see the example on page 78) with pictures of food on a few spaces across it. With a magic marker draw either smiling or frowning faces on the back of the cards. There can be up to six faces per card but all the faces on any one card must be the same. Shuffle the cards thoroughly, but do not mix the two colours together. Then place the two piles of cards in the centre of the board.

PROCEDURE

1 The first child rolls the dice and moves his or her counter. The other children can count the numbers out loud.
2 If the child lands on an empty space, he or she passes the dice to the next child.
3 If the child lands on a space with a food picture the whole group says in chorus *Do you like ... (carrots/apples/chips)?*

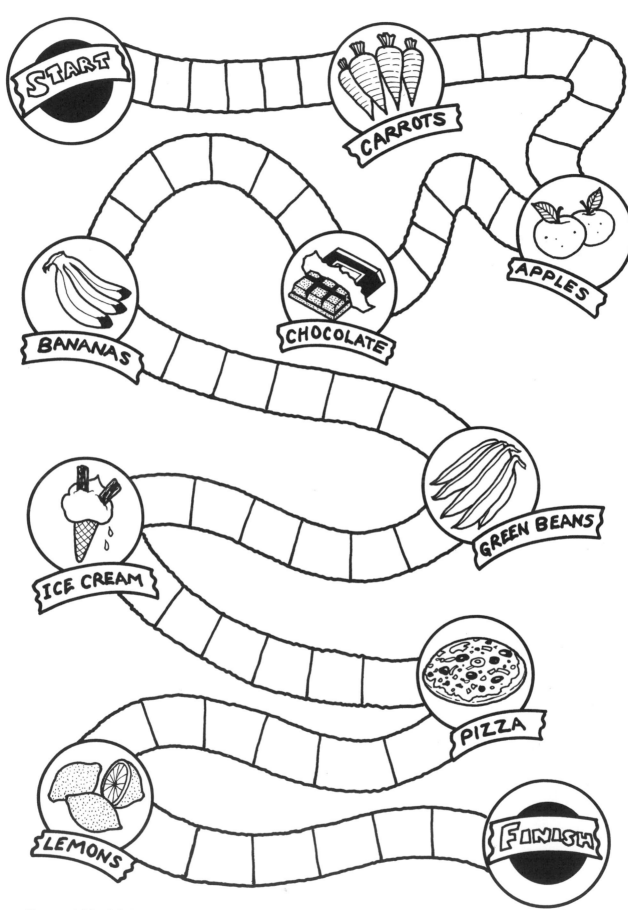

4 The child answers *Yes, I do*, or *No, I don't*. For *Yes*, he or she takes a card from the blue pile; for *No*, from the red pile.

5 The child counts the number of faces on the card. If the faces are smiling, the child moves forward by that number. If they are frowning, the child moves backwards.

6 Continue for about 15 minutes or until each child has had at least one go.

VARIATION 1	Instead of food, use pictures of simple action verbs such as *swim, jump, run, sing*. Substitute *Can you …?* for *Do you like …?* The children can circle the board miming the action. Great fun!
VARIATION 2	Change the theme to toys or body parts + adjectives and practise *Have you got …?* or *Do you have …?*
VARIATION 3	For older children, mix forfeits into the card piles, for example, *Touch something blue* or *When's your birthday?* You could also add more complicated game language such as *Miss a turn* or *Take another card*.
VARIATION 4	Older children can also choose forfeits and help design the game board. Make sure that the forfeits are not mean or disruptive.

6.3 Whisper race

GAME TYPE	**Team game**
AIMS	**Language:** Vocabulary revision (+ any phrase which needs practice); listening carefully.
AGE	6+
GROUP SIZE	10–20
TIME	**15 minutes**
MATERIALS	Three identical sets of 6–10 food cards.
PROCEDURE	

1 You will need a large room for this game. Split the class into two teams. Put one set of cards beside the wall at one end of the room. The teams sit in two lines, with about two metres between each child. The lines should be about the same distance from the cards.

2 Put one set of cards in front of each line of players. The cards must be in the same order.

3 Call *Go!* and the race begins. The first child from each team turns over the top card, for example a pizza. He or she gets up, runs to the next child in the team, crouches down and whispers *Pizza*.

The first child then sits down in the place of the second child, who gets up and runs to the next child.

4 This continues until the last child in the line has heard the word. That child runs to the front and tries to take the pizza card from the set of cards by the wall, before the other team reaches it. Whoever takes the correct card can keep it.

5 The game continues until all the cards have been used. The team with the most cards wins. Referee the game strictly, making sure the children whisper!

VARIATION

Change the theme to any which needs revision.

COMMENTS

You might want to explain how this game works in the children's mother tongue, so that they all understand immediately. If space is tight, have the children crawl instead of running and reduce the distance to the cards.

6.4   Food and poison

GAME TYPE

Card game

AIMS

Language: *This is … Please give me … .*
Other: Decision making.

AGE

8+

GROUP SIZE

6–8

TIME

20 minutes

MATERIALS

A large set of cards with pictures of different food; 'poison' cards (with numbered values of 1–5); (for Variation) pictures from any other theme.

DESCRIPTION

The object of the game is to acquire ten different food cards. Poison cards are the 'strongest' cards. The food cards are the most valuable cards to collect. The other cards have no value.

PREPARATION

Make the cards. You need about 30 food cards, 12 'poison' cards, and 30 other picture cards for a group of six children. The 'poison' cards should be numbered 1–5.

PROCEDURE

1 Shuffle the cards well and deal them out equally to the children.

2 In turn, the children place a card face up on the table, saying *This is a …*

3 If a child plays a 'poison' card, he or she takes all the cards lying on the table. He or she also asks another child for the same amount of cards as the number on the 'poison' card, saying, for

example, *Please give me three cards.* The children should not give away food cards unless they have no choice. Tactically, they should try to wait for the right moment before playing a 'poison' card (for example, when there are a lot of food cards on the table), but before another child plays a 'poison' card. Take the used 'poison card' out of the game.

4 The first child to collect ten different food cards wins. The cards from the other theme(s) don't count.

VARIATION

Change the theme, for example, vehicles and police cars, colours, animals and monsters, etc.

COMMENTS

1 If you don't like the idea of 'poison' or 'monsters', use positive cards, for example, 'love potion', 'magic spell'.

2 With a large class, demonstrate this game first, if necessary in the children's mother tongue, as it is rather complicated, and then split the class into smaller groups.

3 The cards may take some time to make, but they are useful in many different activities.

6.5 Make a menu

GAME TYPE

Card game

AIMS

Language: *I eat/I have ... for breakfast/dinner/lunch.*
Other: Imagination.

AGE

6+

GROUP SIZE

6–8

TIME

15–20 minutes

MATERIALS

60 food cards per eight players. The food should include breakfast, lunch, and dinner, with drinks; (for Variation) a chef's hat.

PROCEDURE

Lesson 1

1 Discuss with the children which food is eaten at breakfast, lunch, and dinner/supper, both in their country and in the UK/US. Practise the language *For breakfast I have ... .*

2 Ask the children to decorate the cards. You can give out templates for them to colour.

Lesson 2

1 Divide the children into groups of 6–8. Mix the cards and deal seven cards to each child. They should not show their cards to the other children. Put the rest of the cards in the middle.

2 Explain to the children that they must group the cards according to meals. There must be at least two cards for each meal. The seventh card can go anywhere (for example, three cards for lunch). Allow the children a short time to sort their cards.

3 In turn, each child can (if they wish) put down three cards and take three more from the pile in the middle.

4 Each child now says their daily menu, practising language such as *For breakfast I have (baked beans)*.

5 When all the children have described their menus, let the group decide on the best one. You can allow some humour here!

VARIATION

Limit the game to lunch or dinner and possibly reduce the number of cards. Compose a festive menu with starters, main course, and dessert. The children should try and 'sell' their meal to the rest of the group. Give them a chef's hat to wear when they describe their meal. They can use phrases like: *For starters we have ketchup soup and as a main course, broccoli in a chocolate sauce*, etc. The crazier the menu, the harder it is to get the class to 'eat' it.

COMMENTS

1 Some food can be eaten at any meal. Different cultures have different customs. Discuss such differences with your class. However, when compiling their own meals, let them be silly— they can eat ice-cream for breakfast or put ketchup on their cornflakes.

2 Be careful in multi-cultural classes not to let the eating habits of individual students be ridiculed.

6.6   May I take your order?

GAME TYPE

Role-play, team, and card game

AIMS

Language: Requests; food; *May I help you? Yes, I'd like … Give me … I'm sorry, we're out of … .*

AGE

8+ (Variation 2: 6+)

GROUP SIZE

6–10

TIME

15–30 minutes (depending on group size)

MATERIALS

Copies of a menu; several sets of cards with pictures of items on the menu.

PREPARATION

1 Make the menus and cards. The menus should have a number of options for each course. (See the examples on page 83.)

2 Arrange the room so that the desks face each other, a few metres apart. There should be four or five desks per group on one side, facing another desk for the cook.

THE ENGLISH RESTAURANT

Breakfast Eggs with Ham
Cornflakes with milk
Bread with honey and jam
Lunch Chicken soup
Chicken sandwich
Tuna sandwich
Cheese sandwich
*all sandwiches with salad and French fries
Dinner **Starters**
Tomato soup
Potato soup
Main courses
Fish with potatoes and salad
Chicken with peas and rice
Spaghetti with meat sauce
Pizza
Desserts
Ice cream — chocolate, banana,
strawberry, vanilla
Apple pie
Drinks wine, water, orange juice,
apple juice, coca-cola

Photocopiable © Oxford University Press

PROCEDURE

1 Divide the class into groups of customers, waiters, and cooks. There should be one cook for every four or five customers and waiters. The customers sit at their desks, each with a menu. The cook sits at the opposite desk with pictures of food. The waiters stand in the middle.

2 Each waiter approaches a customer and asks *May I help you?*

3 The customer responds *Yes, I'd like …* and orders something from the menu.

4 The waiter runs to the cook and says *Give me …*

5 The cook gives the waiter the correct picture and says *Here you are!* If it has already been ordered, the cook says *I'm sorry, we're out of … .*

6 The waiter returns to the customer and gives him or her the card, or says *I'm sorry, we're out of … Can I get you something else?*

7 The winner is the first customer-and-waiter team to get a full meal, or the first cook to get rid of all his or her food. Monitor that all the players use the target language—if they do not, they must return the food.

VARIATION 1	Allow the children to ask simpler questions such as *What can I get you? We haven't got …*
VARIATION 2	Play a non-competitive version. Give the children the situation and allow them to make up the conversation on their own. Monitor them, but do not interrupt unless they get stuck.
VARIATION 3	Instead of a restaurant, you can role-play a store with a customer, a shop assistant, and a delivery person.
VARIATION 4	Instead of cards, use the real items if suitable.
VARIATION 5	See who can order the cheapest or most expensive three-course meal.
COMMENTS	Although it may seem complex, this game is remarkably easy for most children to understand. The phrases should be pre-taught and the children should be comfortable with them before playing. This game aims at fluency, not accuracy, and you should be tolerant of mistakes.

6.7   Fork, knife, spoon

GAME TYPE	**Card game**
AIMS	**Language:** *Can you …? What wins? A fork beats a … .*
AGE	**7+ (Variation 1: 5+)**
GROUP SIZE	**6–8**
TIME	**10–15 minutes**
MATERIALS	About 30 food cards per eight players.
PROCEDURE	1 Show the children the three hand movements:

- a fork (a hand held horizontally, with three fingers spread out)
- a knife (a hand held vertically)
- a spoon (a cupped hand)

2 Explain to the children that:
   - a fork beats a knife
   - a knife beats a spoon
   - a spoon beats a fork.

   For younger children, explain with lots of mime and gesture.

3 Split the class into teams. Each two teams sit in lines facing each other about one metre apart. Between the two teams put 10–20 food cards in a line.

4 The first two players on each team stretch out their hands while the rest of the group chants *fork, knife, spoon, fork, knife, spoon, fork, knife, **spoon***, stressing the final *spoon*.

5 When they hear the stressed *spoon*, the first two players make one of the three hand symbols.

6 Ask *What wins?* Try and elicit *A knife beats a spoon*, etc.

7 The winner can now turn over any card. The rest of the group asks *Can you eat/drink … with a fork/knife/spoon?* If the child can, he or she may take the card. If one cannot eat or drink the food with the chosen utensil, the card is turned back over.

8 Continue with the next two players, until all the cards in the middle have been taken. The team with the most cards wins.

VARIATION 1

With very young children, play the game without the cards. This is the traditional version of the game. Put the children into pairs to play. After each round mix the pairs.

VARIATION 2

Add an element of competition to Variation 1. Each pair play 'best out of three' or 'best out of five'. If this seems too complicated you could say that the 'first to three' is the winner.

COMMENTS

This game is based on the traditional game 'Scissors, paper, stone'.

7 Out and about

Over the years, a child's world grows ever larger and more complex. From the home, they set out to discover the outside world: streets, playgrounds, shops, parks, the doctor, school or kindergarten. Later they learn to place the neighbourhood in cities, towns, or villages, which in turn are in countries—on continents.

As children grow, they move about this world. They remember where things are and how to get to them. They are interested in transport: cars, buses, and trams, aeroplanes and airports, trains and stations. Natural barriers such as mountains, rivers, and oceans and ways to pass them such as bridges and tunnels fascinate them. Authentic material like maps, photos, tickets, foreign coins, add an extra thrill. But children are not only interested in the real world. They are eager to use their imagination and create worlds of their own. They like to design their 'dream house' or the 'city of the future'.

In this chapter, the children learn to give directions in English and describe locations. In doing so they use many common prepositions and practise imperatives. The vocabulary input can be as rich as the worlds you and your children inhabit.

7.1 Rock the boat

GAME TYPE	**Movement game; role play (Variation 2)**
AIMS	**Language:** Directions; imperatives. **Other:** Imagination.
AGE	4+
GROUP SIZE	8–15
TIME	**10–15 minutes**
MATERIALS	A sailor's cap; string or chalk; a picture of a boat and a storm.
PREPARATION	1 Clear a space in your classroom large enough for the children to move around comfortably. This game can also be played outside. 2 Either draw the outline of a boat in chalk on the floor, or make an outline with string. You need one boat for every 15 children.

PROCEDURE

1 Explain to the children that they are going on a boat. Show the picture. You are the captain. Put the hat on your head. Point to the outline of the boat and ask them to step into it.

2 Show the children the picture of the storm. Tell them a storm is coming and that it will 'rock the boat'. Mime the rocking of the boat.

3 Tell the children that they must balance the boat by running 'forward' and 'backwards', 'left' and 'right'. Mime 'balance' by putting your hands out to your sides and rocking from left to right.

4 Go to the front of the boat and call out where the children should move. The children should all do as you say.

5 After five minutes, give a child the sailor's hat and tell him or her to give the commands.

VARIATION 1

You can introduce simple nautical terms such as *fore* (forwards), *aft* (backwards), *port* (left), and *starboard* (right).

VARIATION 2

You can expand the boat idea into a guided fantasy. The children sit with you in the boat. Ask them if the storm is over. Can they see land? Where are they? In America? China? Tell one child to drop the anchor, another to turn on the engines or hoist the sails. Let the children make up their own story.

COMMENTS

Variation 2 can be difficult to keep focused—if so, limit it to five minutes. It can lead on to a craft or other classroom activity on a related theme. (See also 8.8, 'Treasure island'.) For more role-play activities, see *Drama with Children* in this series.

7.2 Mixed-up house

GAME TYPE

Board game

AIMS

Language: Present simple and continuous: *The (couch) goes in the (living-room). I'm moving the (table) to the (dining room). Where's the …?*
Other: Decision making; matching.

AGE

4+

GROUP SIZE

4–10

TIME

10 minutes

MATERIALS

Large playing boards (one per team— see Worksheet 7.2 on page 141); paper; coloured pens; scissors; furniture catalogues; (Variation 1) doll's house and small toy furniture.

PROCEDURE	1 Prepare a large playing board showing the rooms of a house.
	2 The children draw and cut out pieces of furniture and objects usually found around the house. Or bring in pictures cut out from magazines.
	3 Put the furniture and objects in the wrong rooms.
	4 Split the class into pairs or small teams. Each team has to rearrange the furniture and objects, putting them into the right rooms. Note: The children may only move furniture if they say what they are doing in English, for example, *The bed goes in the bedroom*.
VARIATION 1	Use a doll's house and small toy furniture and objects.
VARIATION 2	Other language can also be practised, for example, *The bathtub shouldn't be in the kitchen. Where does the desk go? We're moving a chair to the bathroom.*
VARIATION 3	At the end of each round, the children rearrange the furniture into a new 'Mixed-up house' for the next pair or team.
VARIATION 4	Instead of furniture, the children can put people, animals, or toys in the rooms.
FOLLOW-UP 1	Once the children have played this game a number of times and can use the phrases, let the pairs or teams tell each other where the furniture should go. In this case, each team should have their own house to refer to, as in 7.9, 'Town planning'.
FOLLOW-UP 2	Design a dream house with the children. Each child can furnish his or her own room, and you and the children can work together to furnish the common rooms (kitchen, sitting room, bathroom).

7.3 Obstacle race

GAME TYPE	**Movement game**
AIMS	**Language:** Present continuous; prepositions; classroom objects. **Other:** Physical co-ordination.
AGE	**6+**
GROUP SIZE	**4–10**
TIME	**15+ minutes**
MATERIALS	Chairs; tables; books; other classroom objects; stopwatch; scoreboard.

DESCRIPTION

The object of the game is to go through an obstacle race with various tasks as quickly as possible.

PROCEDURE

1 Set up the obstacles and describe the route to the children. The best way to do this is to go through the obstacles and explain what they are. Possibilities include:
   - crawl under a table
   - hop around a chair
   - balance a book on your head and walk five metres
   - arrange coloured pens in a certain order (for example, as in the rainbow)
   - take off your shoes and socks and put them on again.

2 In turn, the children go through the obstacle course. Time them with a stopwatch. Note down the times on the scoreboard. The fastest child wins.

3 During the actions, each child has to describe what he or she is doing, for example, *I'm crawling under the table*, or *I'm hopping around the chairs*. Alternatively, the other children describe what is happening, for example, *He's running up and down*, or *She's singing a song*.

VARIATION 1

Instead of using the present continuous to describe an action in progress, the children can describe the action before performing it, for example, *I'm going to clap my hands*.

VARIATION 2

Play this game in the gymnasium, perhaps as a combined English and PE lesson, which gives further possibilities for unusual actions, using the equipment there.

COMMENTS

1 The obstacles in the race depend on the possibilities in the classroom, the children's ages and physical abilities, and your and the children's imagination.

2 It is important to keep strict control over this game, especially with larger groups. The children waiting for their turn can hold the stopwatch, write down the times, and referee the child on the course, for example, by watching at various stages of the obstacle course.

3 Children on the course must describe what they are doing in order to finish. The other children describe the actions they are watching.

7.4   Bandits and sheriffs

GAME TYPE	**Movement game**
AIMS	**Language:** *I've got … I've caught …*; classroom objects.
AGE	**6+**
GROUP SIZE	**8–12**
TIME	**15–20 minutes**
MATERIALS	Classroom objects such as erasers and rulers; (for Variation) cuddly animal toys.
DESCRIPTION	The object of the game is for the bandits to 'steal' as many classroom objects as possible, before getting caught by the sheriffs.

PROCEDURE

1 Split the children into two teams. One team are bandits, the other sheriffs. They sit on chairs on opposite sides of a large room. You are the 'Marshall' and stand at the end of the room, next to some empty chairs which are the 'prison'.

2 Give each bandit and each sheriff a number.

3 Place the classroom objects in the middle, but slightly nearer to the bandits. Call out an object and say a number, for example, *Ruler, four*. Bandit number four now runs to get the ruler. At the same time, Sheriff number four chases the bandit.

4 If the bandit manages to pick up the ruler and run back to his or her chair without being 'caught' (touched) by the sheriff, he or she shouts out *I've got the ruler!* The bandits' team keeps the ruler. If a bandit is 'caught', the sheriff shouts *I've caught bandit number four!* Then the sheriff confiscates the ruler and the bandit goes to prison.

5 The game continues until all the classroom objects have been stolen or confiscated, or all the bandits are in prison. The team with the most objects wins. The teams swap roles and play a second round.

VARIATION

Instead of using classroom objects, use cuddly animal toys. The bandits are then the 'hunters', and the sheriffs are 'animal lovers'.

7.5 Directions game

GAME TYPE	**Movement game**
AIMS	**Language:** Giving directions; listening. **Other:** Co-ordination.
AGE	7+
GROUP SIZE	8–16
TIME	**30 minutes**
MATERIALS	Large and small cards; a stopwatch.
PREPARATION	Make about ten large pictures of places familiar to the children. Write the names of the places on ten small cards. The children can help make the picture cards.

PROCEDURE

1 Clear a large empty space in the classroom or play outside or in the hall. Spread the picture cards around the playing area. Mix up the small cards.

2 Divide the class into two teams. Blindfold one child from Team B. The first child from Team A takes a small card and tells the child from Team B how to get to the place shown on it.

3 Time how long it takes the blindfolded child to reach the place. The children can do the timing.

4 After all the children have had a turn, switch the teams around, with Team B giving directions this time.

5 Note down all the times and add them up at the end of the game. The team with the shortest total time for giving directions wins.

VARIATION 1

Buildings and 'Round the Town' are probably the most suitable theme for this game, but you can change to any other theme which needs revising. Try to make the places seem logical to the children. For example, if the theme is animals, the children direct each other to the 'lion's den', the 'bear's cave', or the 'spider's web'. They could also have to imitate the animal, for example crawl like a spider, or jump like a kangaroo.

VARIATION 2

Put cards with traffic-lights, zebra-crossings, roundabouts, etc. around the town. These are 'obstacles' which the children must avoid touching. Add penalties of five or ten seconds if a child touches an obstacle.

COMMENTS

Any game with a blindfold has a certain element of risk. Be absolutely sure that any dangerous objects are removed from the classroom before starting to play. If you have a particularly active, physical class, you could use a map and markers instead of having the children move about.

7.6 Getting around town

GAME TYPE	**Board game**
AIMS	**Language:** *Where is …?* prepositions.
AGE	**7+**
GROUP SIZE	**6–10**
TIME	**30 minutes**

MATERIALS

Game boards; dice; 50 blue and 50 red cards; counters or small picture cards of vehicles (or small toys); (Variation 2) pictures of products available in town.

PREPARATION

1 Design a town game board (see the example on page 93) with various places, such as the post office, supermarket, police station. Colour the remaining spaces on the board alternately red and blue. End the track with a clearly defined finish line. Make one board per 6–10 children. They can help.

2 Prepare 10–20 small red and blue cards for each group. The cards can either have pictures of special places on them, or have instructions to move forward or backward a certain number of spaces, or miss a turn.

PROCEDURE

1 The first child rolls the dice and moves his or her counter or vehicle forward. If the counter lands on a red space, the child takes a red card; if on a blue space, he or she takes a blue card.

2 If child 1 takes a place card, the group chants *Where's the …?* The child now looks at the game board and answers, for example, *The supermarket is on Main Street.*

3 If the answer is correct, the child moves forward to the place on the card. If the answer is wrong, the child does not move.

4 If the place is behind the child's counter, he or she rolls the dice again and moves the counter forward. The child may not take a new card as this could lead to one child having a very long turn.

5 The first child to reach 'finish' wins.

VARIATION 1

Instead of saying *Where is …?* the children give directions. Each card has two pictures or names of places on the town game board, with an arrow pointing from one to the other. The child must answer the question *How do you get from A to B?*

VARIATION 2

Children love to collect things. Prepare cards with pictures of products which they can find or buy at the various places on the board. Hang these products on the wall or blackboard. When a child lands on a place, he or she asks *May I have a …?* If the product can be found at that place, the child wins the card. The child who

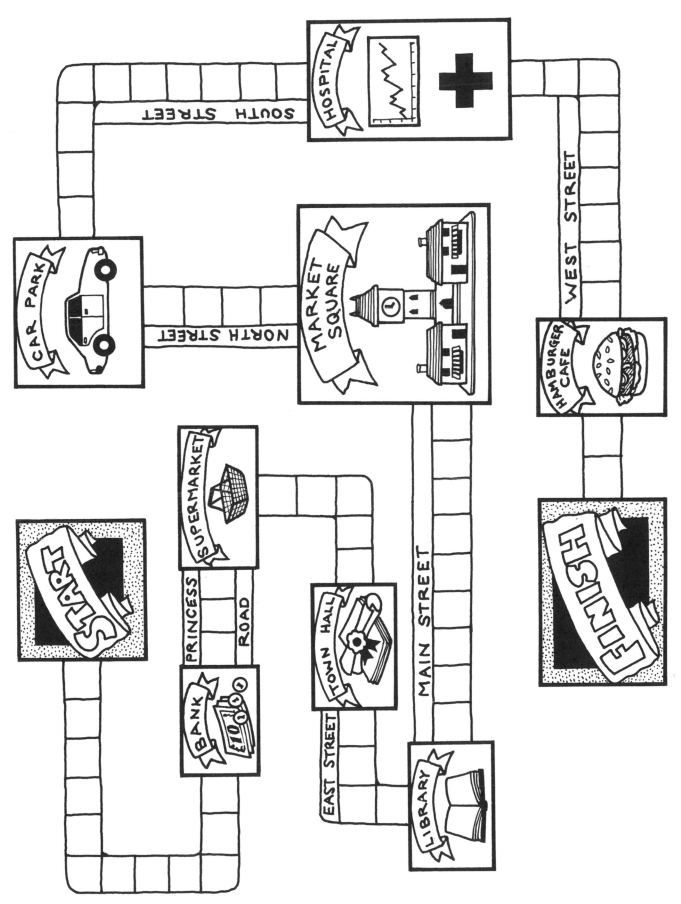

collects the most products wins. There is no need for a 'finish'; the game board can be a square, as in *Monopoly*, with interconnecting roads and routes. Set a prearranged number of rounds or a time limit for this variation.

COMMENTS

Variation 1 is quite difficult for children, so do not be too strict. The aim should be fluency, not accuracy.

7.7   In the house

GAME TYPE

Board or card game; guessing game

AIMS

Language: *Is there …? Are there …? some/any*; basic prepositions: *in, on, under, next to*; house and furniture vocabulary.
Other: Matching.

AGE

7+

GROUP SIZE

8–16

TIME

30–45 minutes

MATERIALS

One card per child with pictures of the rooms of a house with furniture and other contents; a picture of a cross-section of a house showing all the rooms on the cards (see Worksheets 7.2 on page 141 and 7.7 on page 142); a copy of the cross-section for each child; one many-sided dice; pencils and paper.

PROCEDURE

1 Show the children a picture of the cross-section of a house. They should be familiar with the names of the rooms and furniture, but you may want to revise the vocabulary quickly before starting to play.

2 Give each child a copy of the house cross-section.

3 Give each child a copy of a grid like this, or get them to draw one.

Room	Furniture	Name

4 Mix the room cards and give one to each child. This is where the child 'is'. The object of the game is to discover which rooms the other children are in.

5   The children roll a many-sided dice to decide who starts. The highest number begins.

6   The first child looks at the picture of the house and asks any other child a question about his or her room, for example, *Is there a (table/sink)? Are there (chairs/windows)?*

7   If the answer is *Yes*, the child can ask another a question. He or she can ask the same child or another one.

8   If the answer is *No*, the child to the left asks the next question.

9   If a child thinks he or she has discovered who is in each room, he or she calls *Full house!* and play stops. The child must then tell the group who is in each room, for example, *Anna is in the kitchen, Sam is in the bathroom.*

10 If the child is wrong, play continues, but not for very long, since the first player will certainly have revealed where most of the other children are.

VARIATION 1	Make the pictures of each room more complicated, for example, with books on a bookshelf, apples on a table. Put similar pieces of furniture in several rooms. The children must then ask questions with prepositions such as *Is there a cup in the sink?* or *Are there flowers on the table?*
VARIATION 2	Encourage the children to use *some* and *any* in their questions. If the answer is *yes*, the other child must answer with *There is/There are*.

7.8   Passport control

GAME TYPE	**Role-play game**
AIMS	**Language:** To revise as many phrases as possible, for example, *How old are you? I'm … years old. Where are you going? I'm going to … What have you got in your suitcase/bag? I've got … .* **Other:** Role play and imagination; decision-making; maths (currency calculations) for Variation 2.
AGE	**8+**
GROUP SIZE	**4–12**
TIME	**20+ minutes**
MATERIALS	Paper; coloured pens and pencils; cardboard or folders; magazines; (Variation 2) toy money.
PREPARATION	The children make their own 'passports', using paper, pencils, small self-portraits, fingerprints, etc. They also make their own suitcases. Use a folded piece of strong card and either draw in items of clothing, etc., or stick in pictures from magazines. Decorate the

suitcases with pictures showing countries visited, places of national importance, etc. drawn by the children. Add name and address tags. The children can help decide what a passport should look like, what one needs to take in a suitcase, etc.

PROCEDURE

Use the passport as an 'entrance document' to the lesson. Each child has to show you his or her passport before entering the class. You are the passport control officer and ask each child one or two simple questions, for example, *How old are you? Where are you from?* and the children answer. Finish a lesson in the same way: the children have to show their passports and answer questions before they leave the room.

FOLLOW-UP

Make the whole classroom into an 'airport'. The children take the roles of passengers, passport controllers, customs officers, luggage check-in officers, etc. The officers ask questions, and the passengers have to answer. The range of questions and answers which can be practised in this game is unlimited.

VARIATION 1

The suitcases contain clothing, but also gifts (for example, perfume) subject to customs restrictions. If a player has too many gifts, the customs officer can confiscate them.

VARIATION 2

Passengers have toy money and have to travel through different countries on a limited budget. This makes the game competitive. Try involving the children in deciding the rules of the game, for example, what are the customs restrictions? How much money should each child get at the start of the game?

COMMENTS

1 There are no strict rules for playing this game. Be flexible and allow the children to put in their own ideas. Use the game as an introduction to a project on travel. You may need to explain some parts using the children's mother tongue before making and playing the game.

2 Be aware that not all the children will have had the opportunity to travel.

7.9 Town planning

GAME TYPE

Board and team game

AIMS

Language: Simple present tense; prepositions.
Other: Making team decisions.

AGE

8+

GROUP SIZE

6–12

TIME

30 minutes

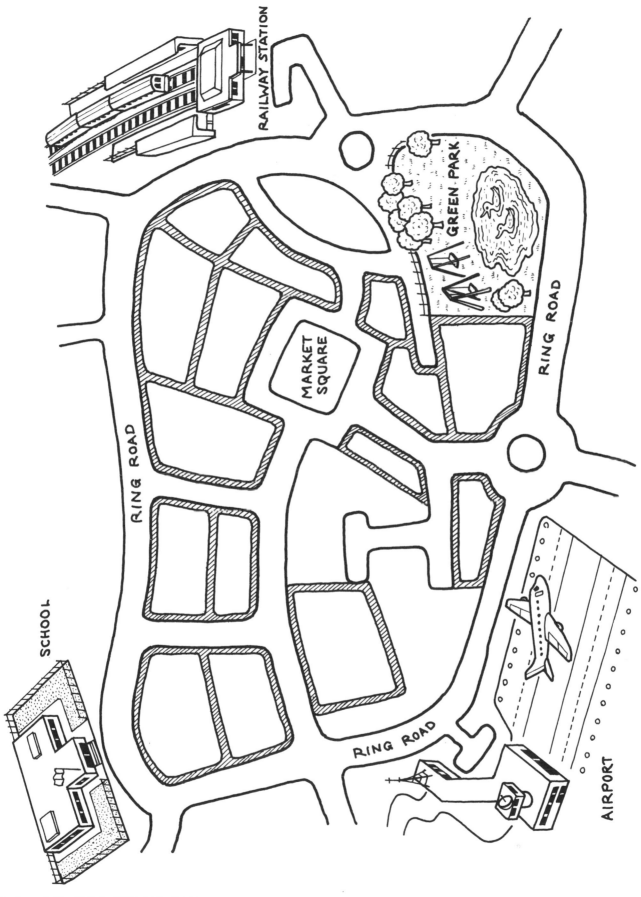

RAILWAY STATION

GREEN PARK

RING ROAD

RING ROAD

MARKET SQUARE

SCHOOL

RING ROAD

AIRPORT

MATERIALS

Maps of a town (see the example on page 97) and identical sets of about 16 small cards of buildings, people, etc. for each team (see the flashcards on page 145).

PROCEDURE

1 Divide the children into teams of 6–12. Give each team a map of a town and a set of flashcards. Lay these face up in front of the teams. The object of the game is to place the cards in the correct position on the map. As this is a competitive game, the teams hide their maps from their opponents, for example, behind a large book.

2 Say where the cards should go, using simple phrases in the present tense, for example, *The cinema is a block north of the restaurant. The bank is next to the flower shop. The doctor lives in a house next to the station. The policeman's got a dog. The nurse lives with her grandmother in a small house opposite the pub.*

3 The children in each team discuss where each card should go and then put them on the map, ideally using Blu-tack to stick them in position. The team with the most correctly placed flashcards wins.

VARIATION 1

Extend this game to include other vocabulary and phrases. Once the children have got used to the game, they can, in turn, do the dictating. You correct any mistakes.

VARIATION 2

The children can make their own maps and flashcards as a craft activity and then use them to play the game.

7.10 Shopping spree

GAME TYPE

Card and dice game

AIMS

Language: *I want to buy this/these … for … dollars. I don't want to buy this/these … because it's/they're too expensive*; numbers.
Other: Making decisions; budgeting.

AGE

8+

GROUP SIZE

4–8

TIME

15–20 minutes

MATERIALS

36 small flashcards per group with pictures of food, clothes etc.; blank cards; dice; counters; toy money.

PROCEDURE

1 Put the small flashcards face-up in a large circle or square. Tell the children that this is a big department store. Give each child 35 dollars (or whatever currency you wish to use). The children should try to buy as many articles as possible with this money.

2 In turn, the children roll the dice and move their counter from card to card. They can move in any direction. They can choose whether or not to buy the card they stop on. It costs as much as the number on the dice; for example, if a player rolls a three, the article costs $3. The player says *I want to buy this ... for $3*, or *I don't want to buy this ... because it's too expensive*. Change the phrases to suit the language level of the children.

3 You play the role of the shop assistant. If a child buys an article, he or she hands the money over and gets the card. Put a blank card in its place.

4 When all the articles have been bought, or when there are only a few articles left, or when all the players have run out of money, the player who has bought the most articles wins the game.

VARIATION 1

With large classes, the children can play in teams or pairs. You may also want all the children to play at once in smaller groups on separate tables.

VARIATION 2

Use large pictures spread around the classroom floor. One member of each team is the buyer and walks along the track of cards in the 'department store'. The other children decide what to buy.

8 Multi-purpose games

Although many of the games in this book can be used to practise a variety of themes, as shown in the variations, multi-purpose games stand out because their basic structure is not language dependent, so they can be used to practise any language.

Because of their flexibility, multi-purpose games are great reserve activities, when another activity isn't working or if you finish too quickly. Once the children have played a multi-purpose game, you can use it again and again without having to explain it. This will reduce your planning time, and have the added advantage of being a safe choice: if your children liked a game, they should enjoy playing it again. Of course any game you play too often will eventually bore the children.

8.1 True/False chairs

GAME TYPE	**Movement game**
AIMS	**Language:** Any. **Other:** Quick reactions.
AGE	**4+**
GROUP SIZE	**8–30**
TIME	**10–15 minutes**
MATERIALS	Two chairs and picture cards or real objects per child; thick piece of coloured string (optional); (for Variation 3) boxes and marbles or beans; bell.
PROCEDURE	1 Put the chairs in two straight lines on either side of the classroom. If the class is too large or the space too tight, draw a line or lay a thick piece of coloured string in the centre of the room, or play outside.
	2 Line up the children in the centre of the room, between the rows of chairs or on the line. Tell them that one row of chairs or one side of the line means 'true' and the other row or side means 'false'. Demonstrate this by showing a flashcard of, for example, a *dog* while you say *cat*. You may need to do this once or twice until the children understand the idea.
	3 Take a flashcard or other prop and say something obviously the opposite or quite wrong. Then hold up a card or object and say

something correct. Don't only use vocabulary. Instead of saying, for example, *bird* when holding up a picture of an elephant, you can say *This animal can fly!*

4 The children decide whether your statement is true or false and sit in the correct row of chairs. Children who choose the wrong row are out.

5 The last child remaining wins.

VARIATION 1	Choose a child to call out the cards. Make sure he or she speaks in English.
VARIATION 2	For advanced children you can read or play a tape of a story they know, but with mistakes. In this variation, the children will only move when they hear something wrong. For very little children, be sure to speak very exaggeratedly when you come to the mistakes. The children should be very familiar with the story.
VARIATION 3	Play this as a competitive team game. On the third side of the room, put a large box of marbles or beans on a table. On the fourth side put a red box and a green box. Each child is a member of the red or green team. Give the children only a very short time—a few seconds—to decide whether what you say is true or false, then ring a bell or clap your hands. The children who go to the correct side of the room take a marble or bean and put it in their team's box. When all the marbles are used up, the team with the most wins.

8.2 Vocabulary scramble

GAME TYPE	**Movement game**
AIMS	**Language:** *I'm a …*; vocabulary revision.
AGE	**4–10**
GROUP SIZE	**6–20**
TIME	**5–10 minutes**
MATERIALS	Pictures of vocabulary items on a theme.
PROCEDURE	1 Put pictures of vocabulary items around the room, on the floor, leaning against tables and chairs, or on the walls. For example, on the theme of Hallowe'en you might include a jack o' lantern, a witch, a pumpkin, a cat, and a spider. The children should already know the words.
	2 Each child stands next to a picture. There should be three or four more pictures than children and only one child may stand next to each.

3 Shout *Switch!* The children run to a different, vacant picture. When they arrive they call out *I'm a spider*, etc. The game continues until the children are beginning to get tired. Keep the pace fast.

VARIATION 1

After a few rounds, get the children to call out their vocabulary items. If a child makes a mistake, he or she has to crawl instead of running to the next card.

VARIATION 2

In turn, the children ask each other *Who are you?* or *What are you?* and answer. Extend this to asking *Who is he/she?* etc.

VARIATION 3

Play the game in pairs, practising plural forms, for example, *We're spiders*.

COMMENTS

This is a fast-moving game where the children use language actively. Use it to get rid of children's excess energy in class.

8.3 Robot action game

GAME TYPE

Movement game

AIMS

Language: Imperatives + any phrases which need practice.
Other: Performing actions simultaneously.

AGE

6+

GROUP SIZE

4–15

TIME

5–15 minutes

PROCEDURE

1 Two children volunteer to be robots and stand at opposite ends of a large room. Give the robots a command, for example, *Walk slowly!* The robots are very obedient and follow the command like a robot, with rigid joints and jerky movements. Give further commands, for example, *Wave an arm!* or *Wiggle your nose!* or *Say 'I'm a Robot'*.

2 The robots don't forget previous commands, but carry on doing them all, until they are doing maybe six or seven different actions simultaneously!

3 When the robots have reached the other end of the room, they stop. Two new children become robots. The two previous robots take over the teacher's role and give the commands. The game continues until all the children have been robot and/or teacher at least once, or until just before the fun begins to diminish.

COMMENTS

This is a simple classroom management game which could be extended to make use of complex language structures.

8.4 Cheerleaders

GAME TYPE	**Word, movement, and chanting game**
AIMS	**Language:** Spelling; careful listening; *Give me a ... What does it spell?*
AGE	**6+**
GROUP SIZE	**4–20**
TIME	**5–10 minutes**
MATERIALS	Pictures of cheerleaders (optional).
DESCRIPTION	In the United States of America, cheerleaders are a popular accompaniment to sports events, especially American football. They are usually a group of boys and girls who wear colourful costumes and chant slogans in support of the competing teams.
PROCEDURE	1 If the children in your class have never heard of or seen cheerleaders, describe them, perhaps in the mother tongue, so that they will understand the idea of this game. Show them the pictures of cheerleaders. The object of the game is to repeat the letters the cheerleader calls and try to guess what they spell.

2 The children stand in a circle. Call out *Give me an A!* The children call *A!* Then call out *Give me a P* (the second letter of the word, for example, *apple*) and so on, until a word has been completely spelled out. You may want to hold up pictures of the objects or actions to be sure that the children understand the meaning of the words.

3 Then ask *What does it spell?* The children call the word, if they can. The first child to call the word correctly becomes the next cheerleader. The game should continue until the fun is not quite exhausted.

VARIATION 1	The game should start with simple, preferably short words, for example, *cat*, *dog*, *pig*, *cow*, *car*, *bus*, and become slowly more complicated.
VARIATION 2	Some actions could be included, like the ones cheerleaders do at sports events. This can make the game even more fun.
COMMENTS	This is a simple repetition game. The children should have a very good knowledge of the alphabet. Use any one topic or various topics in combination.

8.5 One word singing

GAME TYPE	**Singing game**
AIMS	**Language:** Any; rhythm. **Other:** Keeping time.
AGE	**6+**
GROUP SIZE	**4–12**
TIME	**10–15 minutes**
PROCEDURE	1 The children sit in a circle on chairs. Decide on the first song and sing one or two verses together, to get in the mood for the game. 2 In turn, each child sings only one word of the song, for example, Child 1 sings *Old*, child 2 sings *McDonald*, child 3 sings *had*, child 4 sings *a*, child 5 sings *farm*. You may let the children clap to keep the pace and rhythm of the song going. 3 The song continues like this, round the circle, until it is finished. The child who sings the last word can decide what the next song will be. It will take a few rounds of false starts before the children get used to this game.
VARIATION 1	To make the game competitive, a child who sings the wrong word or more than one word is 'out'.
VARIATION 2	If singing only one word is too difficult, allow the children to sing two or three words, or a line of the song.
COMMENTS	This is a fun game and you can use it to practise any songs the children know well. Play it with the children as individuals or in teams.

8.6 What's that card?

GAME TYPE	**Card and guessing game**
AIMS	**Language:** *Is it a/an ..?Yes, it is/No, it isn't/Are they …?/Yes, they are/No, they aren't.* **Other:** Memory training.
AGE	**6+**
GROUP SIZE	**4–10**
TIME	**10 minutes**
MATERIALS	10–12 cards per group on any topic.
PROCEDURE	1 Lay 10–12 cards face down in a line. 2 Point to the first card and ask the first child *What's this?* (If you want to make it easier you can tell the children the topic.) 3 The child tries to guess what the picture on the flashcard is, saying, for example *Is it a car?* Turn the card over. The other children answer *Yes, it is* or *No, it isn't.* 4 If the first child guesses correctly, he or she tries to guess the next card. Continue until he or she guesses incorrectly. Then all the cards are turned face down again and the next child starts guessing from the beginning again. 5 The first child to guess or remember all the pictures wins. Remember what the final card in the line is and don't turn it over until a player really has guessed it correctly.
VARIATION	Use cards with pictures of two or more things. Practise plurals with the phrases *Are they …?Yes, they are/No, they aren't.*

8.7 The fortune teller

GAME TYPE	**Guessing game**
AIMS	**Language:** Future with *will*; question words; *can*; *do*. **Other:** Imagination.
AGE	**6+**
GROUP SIZE	**8–30**
TIME	**Variable**

MATERIALS

A turban and other bright, fun clothes for a costume; some fabric to cover your table; optional: a set of tarot cards, either real ones or your own design; a round glass bowl or ball.

PROCEDURE

1 In a previous lesson, introduce the idea of the fortune teller. Enter the classroom dressed up and go to your seat with dramatic movements and flourishes. In a deep mysterious voice tell the children: *I am the great fortune teller …!* (Use an unusual name.) *I can tell the future. I can tell* your *future!* (Look a child in the eye.)

2 With great ceremony place four tarot cards face down on your table. Turn the first card over. Make an expression of dramatic shock.

3 The children chant *Oh what do you see, great …?*

4 Answer mysteriously, for example, *I see spinach for dinner, but ice-cream for dessert*, or *You will …* Never make the prediction really bad.

5 Repeat the procedure until four cards are turned over.

VARIATION 1

The children ask the fortune teller questions about the future such as *Will I win the tennis match tomorrow? What will I do this summer?* or *Who will I marry?* Put your hand to your forehead, shut your eyes and take a card, then make your prediction.

VARIATION 2

If you have a very large group make predictions for the whole class or even for the country, for example, *Germany will win the World Cup!*

VARIATION 3

Replace *What do you see?* with *What can you see?*

VARIATION 4

After playing this game a few times, more advanced children could take over the role of fortune teller, making the predictions. If you have enough props, split the class into smaller groups with one child from each group taking the role of fortune teller.

COMMENTS

1 In some cultures, fortune telling and magic may be approached only with caution. Find out if the game is suitable before introducing it.

2 The tarot cards are just a prop and do not need to relate to your 'predictions'. You could also use a round glass bowl for a 'crystal ball'.

8.8 Letters and themes dice

GAME TYPE	**Word and dice game**
AIMS	**Language:** Any.
AGE	7+
GROUP SIZE	8–16
TIME	**20–30 minutes**
MATERIALS	Two large dice, one with letters on each face, the other with either names or pictures of themes; (for Variations 2 and 3) two dice with verbs and prepositions.
PREPARATION	If special dice are not available, stick small stickers, available at stationers, on each face of the dice and draw the theme, letter, etc. Otherwise you can make dice using the 'Star Dice' template in Worksheet 2.12 (see page 139).

PROCEDURE

1 Divide the class into two teams.

2 Team 1 rolls the dice and must think of a word beginning with the letter on the first dice about the theme on the second dice. If they are correct, give the team one point and they keep control of the dice.

3 If team 1 answers incorrectly, team 2 has a go. If they answer correctly they get one point and continue rolling.

4 A different child on each team rolls the dice each time. Although the children may confer, the child who rolled must answer the question. Set a time limit of, say, 30–60 seconds for the team to answer.

5 After about ten rounds, the team with the most points wins.

VARIATION 1

Instead of just thinking of single words, each team has to form a sentence using the letters and themes. If the sentence is wrong the other team can correct it and earn a point. They also get control of the dice.

VARIATION 2

Introduce a third dice with verbs or prepositions on each face.

VARIATION 3

If the children are really good, introduce two new dice: one with verbs and one with prepositions. This will reduce the number of turns considerably and is good for groups who like a challenge.

COMMENTS

The dice needn't have only six sides. Alternatively, if suitable dice are not available, make spinners (see the illustration on page 108) or use piles of flashcards.

8.9   What you need quartet

GAME TYPE	**Card game**
AIMS	**Language:** Sports; *What do you need to play ...? I need ... Have you got ...? Do you have ...? Please give me ... May I have ...?* **Other:** Sorting.
AGE	7+
GROUP SIZE	4–6
TIME	**20–30 minutes**
MATERIALS	One pack of cards per group containing 4–6 pictures of sports such as tennis, football, volleyball—at least four cards for each sport with pictures of equipment needed to play (for example, for tennis: tennis ball, racquet, net, court; for football: goal, football, football boots, goalkeeper's gloves). There should always be 50% more cards than children playing.
PROCEDURE	1 Mix the game cards and distribute them to the children. 2 Decide how many equipment cards each child must collect (for example, 4–6), then deal out this number of cards to each child, leaving the other cards in the middle. 3 The first child chooses another child and says *I need a (racquet) to play tennis. Have you got a (racquet)?* 4 Child 2 must answer honestly, saying *Yes, I've got a ...* or *No, I haven't.* 5 If child 2 has the card, he or she must give it to child 1. If not, child 1 takes a card from the top of the pile in the middle. 6 Child 1 must next discard a different card from his or her hand. This card goes to the bottom of the pile in the middle. 7 The first child to collect all the equipment cards for a sport wins.
VARIATION 1	Instead of sports, think of other activities: for example, mailing a letter, cooking spaghetti, going to school.

VARIATION 2	For more advanced children, after step 4 add *May I have …?Yes, you may* or *Can I have …?Yes, you can*, etc.
VARIATION 3	For younger children, have no discard pile but deal out the same number of equipment cards as there are children playing. Instead of putting a card into the middle, child 1 must exchange cards with child 2. If child 2 does not have the desired card, the next child has a turn.

8.10 Make a message

GAME TYPE	**Word and team game**
AIMS	**Language:** General vocabulary and short sentences. **Other:** Quick thinking; imagination.
AGE	8+
GROUP SIZE	4–10
TIME	**10–15 minutes**
MATERIALS	Blackboard; paper and pencils.
PROCEDURE	1 Write a word on the blackboard, for example, H-E-L-I-C-O-P-T-E-R. 2 Split the class into teams of 4–10 children. Each team goes to a corner of the room and tries to write a message, using the letters of the word on the blackboard as the first letters of the message words, for example: **HUNGRY? EGGS LYING IN CUPBOARD! ONE POTATO, TOO! EAT RAW!** 3 The children decide on punctuation. The messages don't have to be grammatically correct as long as the meaning is clear. 4 Give one point for each word a team includes in their message.
VARIATION	This is a rather advanced game for children with a wide knowledge of vocabulary. To simplify it for younger or less advanced children, leave out the idea of a message. Teams think of words beginning with the letters of the word written on the blackboard. Repetitions are not allowed.

8.11 Ransom note

GAME TYPE	**Team game**
AIMS	**Language:** Imperatives; revising vocabulary; reading and writing. **Other:** Cutting and sticking; matching (Variation 3).
AGE	**8+** (Variation 3 for younger children)
GROUP SIZE	**4–25**
TIME	**20–30 minutes** (depending on group size and variation)
MATERIALS	Lots of English-language magazines or newspapers; scissors; glue; blank A4 paper.
PREPARATION	Make a 'ransom note' from newspapers as in the example.

PROCEDURE

1 Divide the class into groups of 4–5. The children sit together at desks around the classroom.

2 Give each group a pile of magazines or newspapers, two pairs of scissors, and some glue.

3 Explain to the groups what kidnapping is. Show them the ransom note you have made.

4 Tell the children they have kidnapped someone and must write a ransom note by cutting out words from the magazines and gluing them on to a piece of paper.

5 The ransom note must not have any English mistakes in it. Otherwise the ransom will not be paid.

6 When a group thinks they have a correct ransom note, they bring it to you. If it is correct, give them a thumbs-up sign. They win the game.

7 If their note is wrong, give them a thumbs-down sign. They must return to their table and try again. Do not tell them the

mistakes—they must work them out or write a new note. Of course it is all right to give them hints. Children who have finished can help the others.

VARIATION 1

Instead of a ransom note, ask the children to write a love letter. Make separate groups of girls and boys. For more fun, have the girls take the boys' role and vice versa.

VARIATION 2

Older children can write funny newspaper headlines. The children can award each other 'wacky points' for them.

VARIATION 3

For younger children you can use very bright colourful magazines with lots of pictures. Ask the children to *find something blue*, or *find something big and yellow*. They should sit in a circle with all the magazines in the middle. Each child may take only one magazine at a time and must return it before taking another. The children cut out what they find and glue it to their sheets of paper. After about 6–8 questions they compare pictures. Hang them on the wall of your classroom if possible.

COMMENTS

1 Although it might not be easy, try to encourage the children in each group to speak to each other in English. Circulate from group to group. Ask questions and guide the conversation if necessary.

2 In evaluating the notes, be tolerant. If a group was particularly ambitious, ignore small mistakes and accept the note.

3 Be sensitive in case some of your class come from places where kidnapping is a real threat—in this case, use the Variations.

8.12 Crossword chains

GAME TYPE

Word and team game

AIMS

Language: Any; spelling and writing.

AGE

8+

GROUP SIZE

4–10

TIME

10–15 minutes

MATERIALS

Photocopies of empty 10 x 10 crossword grids or sheets of squared paper; pencils; rubbers; a scoreboard.

PROCEDURE

1 Split the class into teams of 4–10 children. The object of the game is to create crosswords with long words. Give each team a photocopy of an empty 10 x 10 grid, or let the children draw a grid on squared paper. They write one word, horizontally or vertically, on the grid and score one point per letter, for example,

cat = three points, *elephant* = eight points. Check that the children use correct spelling. If a team spells a word incorrectly, write it correctly on the blackboard for them to copy. In this case, the word scores only one point, regardless of its length.

2 After each team has written one word on the crossword grid, they exchange grids and write another word on the new crossword, using the first or the last letter in the chain. They may only write words horizontally from left to right or vertically from top to bottom, but never diagonally. If a team can't think of a word, they get no points for that round and exchange grids again. The children may use words only once on each grid. You decide whether plurals and names are allowed.

3 When no more new words are possible or when the teams can think of no more words, the game is over. The team with the most points wins.

E	L	E	P	H	A	N	T		
A						R			
S						E			
T						E	G	G	
E								I	
R	E	D						R	
		O						A	
		O						F	
C	A	R						F	
				C	H	E	E	S	E

Red team scores 23 points

Blue team scores 21 points

VARIATION 1

Dictate the theme of the next word, for example, animals, clothes. You should be able to supply possible words for each group if challenged by the children.

VARIATION 2

Once a word is written in the grid, the other team gets five points for saying a sentence with this word. Each sentence pattern may only be used once.

8.13 Wild sentences

GAME TYPE	**Team game**
AIMS	**Language:** Simple present tense; writing. **Other:** Imagination.
AGE	**8+**
GROUP SIZE	**4–12**
TIME	**10–15 minutes**
MATERIALS	Flashcards on various topics; paper and pencils for each team.
PROCEDURE	1 Play this as a team game, with two or more teams.

2 Show the first card to the teams. They go to different corners of the room and try to think of a crazy sentence, using the word on the card. For example, if it's a card with the picture of an elephant: *The elephant rides a bicycle*, or if it's a pizza, *I like pizza with chocolate sauce*. Each team writes their sentence on a piece of paper.

3 The teams now compare sentences. An ungrammatical sentence gets no points. For grammatically correct sentences award one point per word and a 'bonus' of three points for the craziest sentence. You can be the judge, or let the children decide.

4 To avoid very long sentences, the children may not use words like *and*, *but*, or *because*. Set a time limit (for example, 30 seconds) for each sentence.

5 Play this game over a prearranged number of rounds (one round = one flashcard). The team with the most points at the end wins.

8.14 Acrostic crosswords

GAME TYPE	**Word and team game**
AIMS	**Language:** Revising vocabulary; writing and spelling.
AGE	**8+**
GROUP SIZE	**4–8**
TIME	**10–15 minutes**
MATERIALS	Three or four empty crossword grids, 15 x 15.
PREPARATION	Prepare three or four empty crossword grids (15 x 15). The children can also draw the grids on squared paper. In each of these, write one

long word vertically down the middle, for example, ELEPHANT, HELICOPTER, PULLOVER, SUPERMARKET. Photocopy each grid for each team.

PROCEDURE

1 Divide the children into teams. Be sure that each team includes at least one good speller. The teams go to different corners of the room. Give each team a crossword grid. The children discuss in a whisper, so that the other teams don't 'steal' their ideas, and try to think of as many words as possible on the same topic which fit horizontally into the vertical word, for example:

```
S N A K E
        L I O N
C R O C O D I L E
        P A N D A
        H
        C A T
        N
H A M S T E R
```

2 The teams score one point for each correct word. In the above example, the team scores six points. Set a time limit for each crossword. Check the spelling of each word. A word spelt incorrectly scores no points. You might like to put pictures around the room to help the children. You can allow dictionaries if you wish: for example, the *Oxford Picture Power Dictionary* gives words by theme.

VARIATION 1

After finishing each acrostic crossword, the children can try and make sentences with their words, scoring extra points for this. Monitor that the sentences are not only grammatical but logical as well.

VARIATION 2

This can easily be turned into an individual activity. Photocopy one crossword sheet for each child.

8.15 Question and answer search

GAME TYPE

Movement game

AIMS

Language: Questions and answers; reading.
Other: Matching.

AGE

8+

GROUP SIZE

10–20

TIME

20–30 minutes

MATERIALS

Firm cardboard in bright colours cut into strips approximately 15 x 3 cm, laminated if possible; music (optional). You need 10–15 question and answer cards per group.

PREPARATION

On each cardboard strip clearly write a question with the corresponding answer on another strip, for example:

Where do you live?	I live in Berlin.
What's your telephone number?	3453089
Do you speak English?	No, I don't. I speak Spanish.

Keep the colours of the strips random, so that the children cannot match them by colour.

Before class hide the strips around the room. Make it a bit difficult, but not too hard.

PROCEDURE

1 Divide the class into two teams. Show them a strip and explain that there are more hidden around the room. Explain that they will get one point for each strip they find, but five points for each correct question-and-answer pair.

2 Give the children five minutes to search the room. Perhaps play some music in the meantime. Each time children find a strip, they must bring it to their team's table before looking for more.

3 Turn off the music and tell the children to return to their tables. Give them another five minutes to sort their strips and see how many question-and-answer pairs they have.

4 The children read their question-and-answer pairs out loud, while you keep a count of the results on the blackboard.

5 The team with the most points wins.

VARIATION 1

If one team reads an impossible question-and-answer pair, the other team can attempt to say it correctly. If they do, award them three points.

VARIATION 2

Instead of question-and-answer pairs write two halves of sentences on the strips. This could also make multiple combinations possible.

VARIATION 3

For advanced children write parts of a dialogue on each strip. Make enough different strips for at least two distinct dialogues. The children try to put together their strips to create a coherent dialogue. It can be a bit silly as long as it remains grammatical.

8.16   Story game

GAME TYPE	**Card game**
AIMS	**Language:** Any; connectors (*and*, *then*, *but*, etc.). **Other:** Imagination.
AGE	**8+ (4+ for Variation 1)**
GROUP SIZE	**8–12**
TIME	**45 minutes**
MATERIALS	Picture cards showing actions and situations familiar to the children (one and a half times as many cards as there are children); two 'The End' cards; dice; (for Variations) 'Once upon a time' cards; jokers; simple story cassette.

PROCEDURE

1 Divide the class into two teams.

2 Mix the cards and deal one card to each child. Put the remaining cards in a pile in the middle.

3 Each team looks at their cards and tries to put together a story. A story must always end with a 'The End' card.

4 One child from each team rolls the dice to decide which team goes first. If the first team does not already have a story, they discard one card and take a new one from the pile in the centre. The second team can take either the discarded card or a new card from the pile.

5 When one team feels they have a story they call *Ready!* They then have five minutes to organize the story among themselves. Note that a team may not tell their story unless they have a 'The End' card.

6 Each player on the team must tell one episode of the story. If the story is totally illogical the other team can call out *Too silly!* You decide if the story is logical or not. If it does not make any sense, the game continues.

VARIATION 1

Very young children do not have to make up a story, but collect and discard cards until they only have cards on one topic, for example, colours, numbers, or body parts. They must then say what kind of cards they have, for example, *We've got numbers*, or simply *Numbers* for very young beginners. Each child then says what is on his or her card.

VARIATION 2

Before starting, play a tape cassette of a simple story. Play it twice. The children must try to remember the story and rebuild it through the cards. When they think they are ready they retell the story from the cards in their hand.

VARIATION 3	As well as the 'The End' card add a 'Once upon a time' card and a joker. To finish, a story must include both 'Once upon a time' at the start and 'The End' at the conclusion. The joker is a card which allows the children to improvise and create their own episode to fit their story. It is a very valuable card.
VARIATION 4	If you are working with a coursebook which includes a story, you can use that story. This is an excellent revision option. For example, you could include cards with episodes from different chapters in the coursebook.
COMMENTS	This is an activity which aims at fluency. While it my be necessary to guide the children through complex grammar in order to get meaning across, do not interrupt the flow of the story if you can still follow it. Make a note of the mistakes and return to them later.

8.17 Long sentence race

GAME TYPE	**Card and dice game**
AIMS	**Language:** Present simple tense; vocabulary revision; connectors; numbers. **Other:** Imagination.
AGE	8+
GROUP SIZE	4–15
TIME	**15–20 minutes**
MATERIALS	45 small picture cards per group; a large table; dice.
PREPARATION	Make one template of 45 cards and photocopy it for each group. You can glue the pictures to index cards to make them more durable. Six of the cards should show pictures of people. The rest of the cards should have pictures from all the topics that the children know.
PROCEDURE	1 Place the 'people' cards at one end of the table. Lay all the cards face down in a long line around the table.
	2 The first child rolls the dice and counts along the line of cards. If the child rolls a five, for example, he or she turns the fifth card face up. This shows a person. The child says the name of the person, for example, *Jane*. The child rolls the dice again, continuing along the line of cards, and starts a sentence. If the next card is a cat, the child might say *Jane's got a cat*. In this way, the child continues along the line, adding more information to the sentence.
	3 Children who make a mistake must stop, but get points according to how far they went down the line. Tell the children beforehand

what actually counts as a mistake—this will vary, according to their language abilities. Over-strictness will reduce the fun of the game. If a child successfully forms a long sentence and passes card 45, he or she gets the full 45 points.

4 Play the game over two or three rounds and add up the points at the end. The child with the most points wins.

COMMENTS

1 You might specify that a particular phrase, for example, *has got*, may only be used once in a sentence, to avoid repetition.

2 Be aware that slower learners might take too long to make their sentences. In a mixed ability class, pair the children up, so that brighter ones can help slower learners. You can also write key words or phrases on the blackboard.

8.18 Treasure Island

GAME TYPE

Board game

AIMS

Language: Any.
Other: Imagination; drawing.

AGE

8+

GROUP SIZE

4–8

TIME

60 minutes

MATERIALS

A large playing board (for example A2); 40 small red and 40 small green cards; dice; a counter for each player.

PREPARATION

1 You can make the game board yourself or prepare it with the children as a craft activity in class. On the board draw a large island surrounded by water, with forests, lakes, and various dangers, for example, quicksand, sharks, spiders, cannibals' village. Draw a track around the island with 60–80 spaces. It should have a start and a finish. On the track mark about 20 'tools' spaces, 20 'treasure' spaces and 20 'danger' spaces, which should be next to the 'danger' pictures on the board.

2 On the red cards, draw about 40 treasures, for example, gold, silver, chest of diamonds, and on the green cards draw about 40 tools, for example, sword, net, ladder, poison, love potion, shot gun. There should be a common denominator for the treasure cards, for example, two pieces of silver = one piece of gold, a chest of diamonds = five pieces of gold, so that it is possible to work out how much treasure each child has at the end of the game. There should be a maximum of eight different types of tool and eight different types of danger.

PROCEDURE

1 Children love the fantasy world of a 'Treasure Island'. Introduce the language and theme by talking about it, telling a story, watching a film, acting, drawing. The children will also need a sound knowledge of game-playing terms to make effective use of this game.

2 In turn, the children roll the dice and move around the board from start to finish. If they land on a tool space, they take a tool card. If they land on a treasure space, they take a treasure card. If they land on a danger space, they must give up the necessary tool card. For example, to get out of quicksand you need a rope, to get over the snake pit you need poison or a ladder. If they do not have the necessary tool card, they must roll the dice again and move backwards along the track.

3 The children should continually be using phrases they know, for example, *I've got a* … . When a child has reached the finish, he or she gets a bonus of three treasure cards. Add up the treasures for each child. The one with the most wins. Tools are worth nothing at the end of the game, but can be bought, sold, and bartered during the game, to increase the language usage.

COMMENTS

This game has many possibilities. You can link it with the guided fantasy in 7.1, 'Rock the boat': the children get shipwrecked on the Treasure Island. It can be part of a project on Pirates—see *Projects with Young Learners* in this series.

9 Old favourites with a new twist

Teaching English to children is still a young field and materials writers are just catching up with teachers' needs. So, many teachers use modified English mother-tongue activities in their TEFL classrooms. There is nothing wrong with this. In fact, using such authentic materials is especially motivating for children. They are excited by the 'real thing'.

But modifying materials takes time and is not easy if you are not confident of your own English-language skills. We have selected twelve classic games which children seem to like and reworked them for young language learners. You will probably recognize many of them. There are lots more we could have included. Perhaps this chapter will inspire you to play with other old favourites of your own.

Unfortunately, materials writers and teachers do not always exploit a game's full potential. We hope the variations of each game in this section give 'old meals new spice'. These new twists can turn something 'old hat' into a new and exciting game.

9.1 Memory (Pelmanism)

GAME TYPE	**Card game**
AIMS	**Language:** *Is this …? Yes, it is/No it isn't; this/these.* **Other:** A good memory; observation; matching.
AGE	**4+**
GROUP SIZE	**6–8**
TIME	**15–20 minutes**
MATERIALS	One set of picture cards per group with at least ten picture pairs (20 cards in all); small cards; magazines; children's glue and scissors (if the children are to make the cards).
PREPARATION	Children like making their own cards. If you choose this option, they should make their cards in a previous lesson. They can either draw pictures on index cards or cut out pictures from magazines.
PROCEDURE	1 Introduce the vocabulary on the cards before playing the game.

2 Shuffle the cards and place them face down in a grid form. For example, if you have 20 cards, place five cards across and four cards down.

3 Child 1 turns two cards face up and says, for example, *This is a (pizza) and this is a (hamburger)*.

4 If the two cards match, the child can keep the pair and have another turn.

5 If the cards do not match, the child puts the cards face down again and the next child turns over two cards.

6 The child who collects the most pairs wins.

VARIATION 1	For the youngest age group, instead of finding pairs the teacher says: *Find an elephant.* The child turns over a card. The teacher asks *Is this an elephant?* The child must say *Yes, it's an elephant*, or *No, it's not an elephant, it's a snake*, or just *Yes, it is* or *No, it isn't*. The children can also tell each other which card to find.
VARIATION 2	Instead of pairs, the children look for cards from a common topic: for example, *nose, mouth, ear, eyes* (face) or *fork, knife, spoon, plate* (eating utensils).
VARIATION 3	Look for opposites instead of identical cards: for example, black–white, old–young, happy–sad, tall–short.
VARIATION 4	Use cards with plurals too so that the children must say *This is …* or *These are … .*
VARIATION 5	In Step 3 combine the two sentences with *but* or *and*: *This is a hamburger but that is a pizza*, or *This is a hamburger and that is a hamburger too.*
VARIATION 6	With older children, use a set of 30 cards with three pictures the same. The children have to find three cards with the same picture or idea.
COMMENTS	With the youngest children, place the cards face up and allow the children to study them for a few minutes before turning them back over and starting the game.

9.2 Bingo

GAME TYPE	**Board game**
AIMS	**Language:** *Is this …? Yes, it is/No it isn't; this/these; have got;* vocabulary revision; listening. **Other:** Matching, simple addition (Variation 1).
AGE	4+

GROUP SIZE	4–12
TIME	**20–30 minutes**
MATERIALS	Paper; coloured pencils; counters (can be noodles or dried beans); a box; 15 different pictures on the same theme; (for Variation 1) four dice; (for Variation 2) coloured dice.
PREPARATION	Draw a large 3 x 3 grid and make one copy per child. Older children can draw their own grids.

PROCEDURE

Lesson 1

1 Hang the pictures on the walls of your classroom.

2 Give out the grids. Ask the children to draw pictures in the spaces—a different picture in each space. They must choose from the pictures on the wall.

Lesson 2

1 You are the caller. Put the pictures in a box and mix them. Pull out one and show it to the children, saying *This is a … .*

2 The children look at their grids and see if they have the picture. If they have it they say *I've got a …* and cover the space with a counter.

3 The first child to cover all the spaces on his or her grid wins.

4 The winner becomes caller. The other children can exchange their cards.

VARIATION 1

The children write numbers between 4 and 24 in the spaces on their grids. In turn, they roll the four dice, add up the points, and say: *The number is … .* Children who have that number on their card call out: *I've got a/an …* and put a counter on the space.

VARIATION 2

Make Variation 1 more complex by using a coloured dice (six colours) in combination with three or four numbered dice. In this version the children draw their numbers on the bingo cards using coloured pencils. These must correspond to the colours on the dice.

VARIATION 3

Increase the size of the bingo board, for example with a 5 x 5 grid. The children must try to get a line of counters, either vertically, horizontally, or diagonally.

9.3 Fruit salad

GAME TYPE	Movement game
AIMS	**Language:** Vocabulary revision; listening; greetings and introductions (Variation 1). **Other:** Quick reactions.
AGE	4+
GROUP SIZE	10+
TIME	**10 minutes**
MATERIALS	At least one card per child with pictures of objects or people, or written words (for older children).
PREPARATION	Clear a large space in the classroom and put one chair per child in a circle. If you don't have chairs, the children can sit in a circle on the floor.

PROCEDURE

1 Put the cards in a box. Move from child to child and let each one take a card out of the box.
2 Call out two words which are on the cards.
3 The children with the two words on their cards stand up and change places.
4 Continue calling out words until all the children have had a chance to change places at least once.
5 After a few rounds more, call *Fruit salad!* or any other phrase that fits in with what you are teaching. (*Hurricane* or *tornado* are good options.) Everyone must get up and change seats.

VARIATION 1

Instead of vocabulary items each card has a picture of a person on it. They can be people the children know personally or famous people, rock musicians, movie stars, cartoon characters or sports personalities. When you call out two names, the children must get up and greet each other saying, for example, *Hi! I'm Donald Duck. What's your name?* The other child can reply *I'm Ronaldo. How are you?* They then change places. You can use any phrases such as *How old are you?* or *Where do you live?* Instead of calling *Fruit salad*, call out something fitting the theme, for example, *Nice to meet you.* The children must all stand up and mingle, shaking hands and greeting each other, and then find a new place to sit down.

VARIATION 2

For older children, write opposites on the cards, for example, *old/young, long/short, happy/sad.* In this variation call out only one word of the pair. The children must look for their opposite and the two change places as in the traditional version.

VARIATION 3   Stand in the middle and try to get a seat when you shout *Fruit salad* and all the children change places. The child without a seat becomes the new caller.

COMMENTS   This game lives from its energy. Keep the pace fast but always allow enough time for everybody to get up and move around when you call *Fruit salad*. This is especially important in Variation 1, where the children need time to mingle and introduce themselves to each other.

9.4   Blind man's bluff

GAME TYPE   **Movement and guessing game**

AIMS   **Language:** *Are you …? Yes, I am/No, I'm not. My name is … .*
Other: Recognition.

AGE   5+

GROUP SIZE   6–10

TIME   **15–20 minutes**

MATERIALS   A blindfold; music (optional).

PROCEDURE
1 The object of the game is to guess the name of a child, by touching but not seeing him or her. Clear a wide open space in the classroom or play outside.
2 The children stand in a large circle. Blindfold a child, who stands in the middle.
3 Tell the other children to walk or dance around, keeping in the circle. You can play music or get the children to sing.
4 The child in the middle calls *Stop!* The other children remain as still as statues. The blindfolded child now approaches one of the other children and touches him or her, feeling hair, pullover, jeans, shoes, etc. Make sure the children do this carefully. The blindfolded one then guesses the other child's name by asking *Are you Jane?* The child answers *Yes, I am* or *No, I'm not. My name is Mary*, etc.
5 If the blindfolded child guesses correctly, the other child now gets the blindfold. If the guess is not correct, the blindfolded child must approach another child. Make sure the children say the phrases and that they all have a turn at being blindfolded. With larger classes, make two or more groups.

VARIATION 1   With a group of 10–15 children, blindfold two or three children simultaneously. This increases the pace of the game and can be great fun.

VARIATION 2	Tell the first child who to find, for example, *Please find Paul!* In this version, the blindfolded child must ask all the children he or she approaches *Are you Paul?* until Paul is found. This is a clever way to practise *No, I'm not.* The children can also tell each other who to find.
VARIATION 3	Change *Are you …?* to *Is your name …?* with the answers *Yes, it is/No, it isn't.*
VARIATION 4	Change the theme, for example, to body parts or clothes and colours. Say *Find somebody with blue eyes. /Find a child with green socks*, etc. The blindfolded child asks *Have you got blue eyes?* etc.
COMMENTS	1 As the object of this game is to discover identity, it is important for the children to understand that if they laugh or squeal or talk during the game, they will easily be found out. With younger children, this is rather difficult to control. With older children, try introducing a points system, for example, a child gets one point if not discovered when touched, but the blindfolded child gets three points for discovering the identity of a child straight away. This helps to calm the children. 2 Be aware that some children do not like being blindfolded. Try encouraging them to join in, but do not force a reluctant child to wear a blindfold.

9.5 Kim's game

GAME TYPE	**Guessing game**
AIMS	**Language:** Classroom objects; *What's missing?/Is it the …? Yes, it is/No, it isn't.* **Other:** Memory training; observation and recognition.
AGE	5+
GROUP SIZE	5–10
TIME	**10–15 minutes**
MATERIALS	At least seven different objects (or picture cards); a cloth; a bag; a tray.
PROCEDURE	1 Sit in a circle with the children. Ask them to give you something of theirs, for example, a pencil. Add keys or other items of your own. There should be between seven and ten objects altogether. Put them in the middle on a tray. 2 Hold up each item and ask *What's this?* Practise saying the words, first each child individually and then in chorus, until the children have a good knowledge of all the items.

3 Cover the objects with a cloth. Ask one child to stand up and turn around. Remove one object from under the cloth, show it to the other children, and hide it in the bag.

4 The standing child turns around again. Remove the cloth and ask the child *What's missing?* He or she replies by asking, for example, *Is it the watch?* The other children chant *Yes, it is* or *No, it isn't.*

5 Each child in turn tries to guess what's missing.

VARIATION 1

After playing one round, ask the children as a group to try to recall all the objects under the cloth. Practise the phrases *There is …/ There are … .*

VARIATION 2

Ask older children to write down or draw as many objects as they can remember. Try using 15–20 objects, which makes it more challenging. Play this variation in teams. They score two points if they remember the word, but only one point if they don't remember the word but can draw the object.

VARIATION 3

Let the children, in turn, take away the objects and ask each other *What's missing?* Make the game more challenging by allowing the children to take away two or three objects. They will also love to take away objects and ask **you** what's missing!

VARIATION 4

1 Take a number of the more sturdy objects (not a watch or pair of glasses) and play a simple but funny passing game. Hold up one object and say *This is a ball.* Pass the ball to the child on your left, who also says *This is a ball.* This child passes it on to his or her left-hand neighbour and so on until the ball comes back to you.

2 In the second round, pass the ball again and a few seconds later, when the ball has already reached at least the second child to your left, pass a second object.

3 In each round, keep introducing one more object, until all the children are passing objects and saying *This is a …* simultaneously. Make sure the children continue to say *This is a …* and not just the word.

4 To make the game even more wild, send objects in both directions! Another possibility is for the children to ask a return question, for example, *This is a ball. What is it? It's a ball.*

VARIATION 5

When the children are used to Variation 4, try playing it with pairs of objects of the same kind, practising plurals and the phrase *These are … .* This can be modified to practise other language structures. It's more suitable for older children (8+) and usually gets rather hysterical!

VARIATION 6

Give each child one object. The children pass round all the objects simultaneously, counting or saying a rhyme or chant at the same time. When you reach number ten, or at the end of the rhyme, shout *Stop!* In turn, the children quickly say, *I've got a … .*

| COMMENTS | Make sure that the children handle each other's things respectfully. You could keep a list of what belongs to who. |

9.6 Beetle drive

GAME TYPE	**Dice and drawing game**
AIMS	**Language:** *I've (already) got … I can draw …* etc.; numbers. **Other:** Drawing.
AGE	**5+**
GROUP SIZE	**5–10**
TIME	**10–20 minutes**
MATERIALS	Paper; coloured pencils; dice; (for Variation 4) 'Mr Muddleman' torso and body parts cut out of strong card.
PREPARATION	Draw a large beetle (see the example on page 128). Label the head 1, the body 2, the legs (left and right) 3 and 4, the two front feelers 5, and the eyes 6. Hang your beetle picture on the blackboard or wall for all the children to see.

PROCEDURE	1 Give each child a piece of paper. Put the coloured pencils in the middle.
	2 In turn, the children roll the dice, saying, for example, *I've got a four. I can draw three right legs*, etc. The child then draws the appropriate parts of the beetle body on his or her paper.
	3 If children roll the same number again, they say, for example, *I've got a four again. My beetle has already got three right legs*, and wait until the next round.
	4 The first child to complete a beetle drawing wins. Let all the children finish drawing their beetles without rolling the dice.

VARIATION 1	Use this game for learning the parts of the human body and clothes. Draw a man or woman and label arms 1, legs 2, head 3, body 4, hands 5, and feet 6. Let the children draw in facial features, hair, etc. Then play the same game with clothes. The children draw items of clothing (for example hat 1, shoes 2, pullover 3, trousers 4, belt 5, and scarf 6) on a separate piece of paper, which they can cut out to dress their man or woman. Allow much more time for this variation.
VARIATION 2	Change the theme to parts of vehicles (for example, draw a car and label wheels 1, boot 2, bonnet 3, doors 4, roof 5, exhaust-pipe 6) or any other suitable theme.
VARIATION 3	Use two dice, increasing the number of parts.

VARIATION 4	**Mr Muddleman Game**

1 Make a large torso of 'Mr Muddleman' and lots of body parts, cut out of strong card. You can do this with the children.

2 In pairs, the children take turns to put the body parts in the right place. Blindfold one child. The other children give directions, for example, *left*, *right*, *up*, *down*, without saying what the body part is. Each pair of children gets one point for each correctly placed body part.

A variation of this fun game is simply to put a body part in the wrong place on Mr Muddleman. The children say, for example, *That's not an eye, it's an ear*, and move the body part into the right place.

FOLLOW-UP

When playing Beetle drive, ask the children to describe their finished pictures at the end of the game, using one or two simple phrases. Older children can also compare each other's pictures. This increases the language production and learning value of the game.

9.7 What's the time, Mr Wolf?

GAME TYPE

Movement and chanting game

AIMS

Language: Telling the time.
Other: Quick reactions.

AGE

6+

GROUP SIZE

6–10

TIME

5–10 minutes

MATERIALS

(Variation 5) Small cards with pictures of chicken grain, or beans.

PROCEDURE

1 The object of the game is to avoid getting caught by the 'Wolf'! Explain to the children that they are the 'chickens' and you are the 'Wolf'. Play in a large open space in the classroom or outside.

2 The chickens stand at one end of the room in a line with one hand on the wall. You stand about two metres in front of the chickens with your back to them. The chickens chant in chorus *What's the time, Mr Wolf?* or simply *What's the time?*

3 Take one step forward and say a time, for example *It's one o'clock!* Now the chickens also take one step forward and ask again *What's the time, Mr Wolf?* The game continues in this way until you decide to say *It's dinner-time!*

4 The chickens turn around and run back to the wall as quickly as possible. You try to catch as many chickens as you can, by touching them before they reach the wall. All 'caught' chickens are out. The last chicken to survive wins.

VARIATION 1	The chickens repeat what the wolf says. This is an ideal way of introducing more complex time-telling structures, for example, *It's half past three*.
VARIATION 2	If you catch a chicken, that child becomes the new wolf, which avoids both competition and boredom amongst the children who are 'out'. Whoever becomes the wolf also has to say the times, increasing language production.
VARIATION 3	To increase the pace of the game, chickens who are caught become wolves. The wolves stand in a line in front of the chickens, taking turns to say the times. This is a good way to play the game with more children.
VARIATION 4	Practise adjectives, for example, *Are you hungry, Mr Wolf? No, I'm thirsty/sleepy/happy/sad/lazy*. Instead of saying *It's dinner-time*, say *Yes, I'm starving!*
VARIATION 5	Inevitably, chickens will try to cheat by not following the wolf or by taking very small steps forward. Make the game more complex and encourage children to take risks by dropping small cards with pictures of chicken grain (perhaps with different points on) or beans along the way. The chickens try to collect these but at the same time try to avoid getting caught. Encourage the chickens to keep on asking *What's the time, Mr Wolf?*
VARIATION 6	An alternative way of keeping the game fair is for you to referee the movement of the chickens, whilst one of the children is the wolf.

9.8   Simon says

GAME TYPE	**Movement game**
AIMS	**Language:** Listening; imperatives; action verbs; prepositions.
AGE	**6–9**
GROUP SIZE	**6–25**
TIME	**10 minutes**
MATERIALS	Optional: flashcards; small objects (fruit, writing utensils, clothing, etc.); (for Variation 2) hats.
PROCEDURE	1 Clear a space in the classroom. The children stand facing you in a large semicircle with enough space to move comfortably. You stand a few metres away from them, so that they can all see you. 2 Call out a command such as *Simon says: touch your nose*. 3 The children must do what you say.

4 Call out a second command, for example, *Clap your hands*, this time leaving out *Simon says*. If children do the action they are out.

5 The last child left in the game becomes the new caller.

6 Join the children in the semicircle and perform the new caller's commands. The children will particularly like it if you make mistakes and get called out. You can monitor the rest of the game.

VARIATION 1	With large groups or those who tend to be hard to control, children should not be out of the game when they make a mistake. Just laugh and keep on playing. Alternatively, have a row of chairs at one end of the classroom. Children who are out have to sit on a chair. You can sit next to the noisy children.
VARIATION 2	Children who are out wear a hat for the next round or perform some kind of fun forfeit. In the next round other children will make mistakes and no children will be stigmatized as 'losers'.
VARIATION 3	Turn 'Simon says' into a team game. The last team with players still in wins.
VARIATION 4	Call out instructions such as *Touch something blue* or *Find a book*. The children scatter throughout the room looking. Children who make a mistake are out. This option is also helpful for practising prepositions, for example, *Sit under the table*, or *Put a book on the teacher's desk*.
VARIATION 5	When the children are used to the game, start including 'wilder' commands to increase the level of fun, for example, *Simon says: put a finger in your ear. Hop around the room. Sing 'Old McDonald had a farm'*. Have the children do all of these actions simultaneously!
VARIATION 6	For the very young (4–6) say *Please* instead of *Simon Says*—the children should only do the action if you say *Please*.
COMMENTS	'Simon says' must be played at a fast pace. In principle, you can add the Simon says idea to any game you choose, to make it more difficult or simply to give it a new twist.

9.9 Cat and mouse

GAME TYPE	**Movement game**
AIMS	**Language:** *Can I...? No, you can't*; telling the time; listening.
AGE	**7+ (4+ for Variation 1, 8+ for Variation 4)**
GROUP SIZE	**8–20**
TIME	**15–20 minutes**

MATERIALS

Strips of paper and a box (for Variation 4).

PROCEDURE

1 The children stand in a circle, holding hands, with their arms down.

2 One child stands in the centre of the circle. This child is the mouse. Another child stands outside the circle. He or she is the cat.

3 The cat taps the shoulder of any child in the circle and asks *Can I come in?*

4 The child in the circle replies *No, you can't.* The cat then asks *When can I come in?*

5 The child in the circle then says a time, for example, *At six o'clock.*

6 The children in the circle begin chanting *One o'clock, two o'clock, three o'clock …* until they reach the time that the cat is allowed to enter. They then raise their hands in the air.

7 The cat now enters the circle while the mouse runs out the other side to escape. The mouse runs around the outside of the circle chased by the cat.

8 If the mouse runs around the circle three times without being caught, he or she goes back into the middle and the children put their arms down again. A new child now becomes the cat.

9 If the cat catches the mouse, the cat becomes the new mouse and goes inside the circle. The former mouse joins the circle. Choose a new child to be the cat.

VARIATION 1

Play the game without 'telling the time' language. In this case, the children in the circle dance around the mouse and chant *One, two, three! The mouse is free!* and then lift up their hands.

VARIATION 2

The children in the circle sing a song they all know and enjoy. After the cat taps one child on the shoulder, the circle continues singing until the child lifts his or her hands and calls out *The mouse is free!*

VARIATION 3

Combine 'Cat and mouse' with another old favourite, 'Johnny may I cross the water?' In this version the cat taps a child and asks *Can I (May I) come in?* The child responds *Only if you … (touch your nose, count to ten, hop ten times, say all the children's names,* etc. Whenever possible let the children decide what the cat should do, but monitor them closely so they don't request anything impossible or embarrassing.

VARIATION 4

For older children, write instructions on strips of paper and put them in a small box. When the cat taps a child, he or she chooses a strip of paper from the box and reads it to the cat. If the cat performs the action correctly, the children lift their hands and the chase can begin.

| COMMENTS | If a mouse is not caught after three rounds, choose a new mouse so that all the children have a chance to play. |

9.10 Draw, fold, and pass

GAME TYPE — **Drawing game**

AIMS — **Language:** *He's got … She's got …*; present continuous; descriptions; colours, numbers, clothes, etc.
Other: Drawing; folding paper; imagination.

AGE — 6+

GROUP SIZE — 4–12

TIME — **10 minutes**

MATERIALS — A4-sized paper; coloured pencils.

DESCRIPTION — This game is great fun because it lets the children use their imagination and be creative at the same time. It is not a competitive game. The object is to draw crazy people or monsters and afterwards describe them.

PROCEDURE

1 Give each child a piece of paper. Put the coloured pencils in the middle.

2 You should play too, showing the children how to draw the pictures. First draw a head. Then fold the page back at the base of the head. Everyone passes their paper to the person on the right.

3 Draw the next part of the body (this can be the neck, shoulders, etc.) and fold the papers back again. Pass them on again.

4 The drawing game continues in this way until the feet and toes have been drawn. As this is a creative game, you can draw almost anything, for example clothes, five arms, hands holding things.

5 When all the pictures are finished, unfold them to reveal the crazy creations. In turn, the children describe the pictures using all the phrases they know.

VARIATION — Change the theme of the pictures to crazy vehicles, buildings, etc. or combine themes, for example monsters with 'normal' and mechanical body parts (wheels instead of feet, etc.).

COMMENTS — The children need to fold the paper in the proper place and as neatly as possible. You may want to help younger children.

9.11   Back writing

GAME TYPE	**Word and guessing game**
AIMS	**Language:** Spelling; word recognition; *I think you're writing .../ Yes, I am/No, I'm not. It's ... Yes, it is/No, it isn't.*
AGE	**8+**
GROUP SIZE	**3–6**
TIME	**10 minutes**
MATERIALS	Scoreboard.

PROCEDURE

1 The object of the game is to recognize words written on your back. The children should have a good knowledge of spelling.

2 The children sit in a line at one end of the room. Child 1 stands a few metres away with his or her back to the other children. Child 2 walks up to child 1 and starts writing a three- or four-letter letter word on his or her back, using a finger as a pen. Child 2 should write firmly enough for child 1 to be able to feel the letters. The children should write each letter slowly and individually. If necessary help the children by writing a large selection of three- and four-letter words they know on the blackboard.

3 As soon as child 1 thinks he or she knows the word, he or she calls *Stop!* and says *I think you're writing CAT!* Child 2 answers *Yes, I am,* or *No, I'm not.* If a child guesses the word correctly before the writer has finished, he or she gets three points. If the child guesses correctly after the word has been written once, both children get two points (this encourages clear writing). If the word has to be written a second time, they only get one point for a correct guess. If after two tries the child has still not guessed, the writer says what it is.

4 The next child has a turn. The game finishes when all the children have been writers and written on at least once. The child with the most points wins.

VARIATION

The children have to say which topic the word belongs to before writing, for example, *This word is an animal.*

COMMENTS

With larger classes this game is best played in small groups of three children. In each turn, one child is the writer, one child is written on, and the third child referees the turn. Naturally you should demonstrate two or three times in front of the whole class before the groups play on their own.

9.12 Categories

GAME TYPE	**Guessing game**
AIMS	**Language:** Questions and answers; numbers.
AGE	**8+**
GROUP SIZE	**8–10**
TIME	**30–45 minutes**
MATERIALS	Magnet board, felt board, or blackboard; question cards; stopwatch; horn or buzzer.
PREPARATION	1 Draw 4–6 vertical columns across the board (see the example). Each column should represent a theme. Either write the theme or draw a picture for small children. Themes could include numbers, colours, body parts, or animals.

2 Divide each column into five squares of equal size. Number the squares in each column *10, 20, 30, 40, 50*. Each square represents a question.

3 The questions get progressively more difficult. A question for 10 could be *What animal says woof-woof?* A question for 30 could be *This animal has a trunk.* (The children must guess the animal.) A question for 50 can be especially challenging, for example, *Sing a song about animals.*

PROCEDURE

1 Divide the class into pairs. The children give their pair a name and write it on a cardboard sheet folded in half. The pairs sit together at desks, in a semicircle. You stand in the front at the board.

2 One child in the first pair chooses a theme and number, for example, *We would like animals for 20*. (Just *Animals for 20* will do for younger children.) You take a number 20 card from the animal question pile and read the question on it.

3 Each pair has approximately 30 seconds, or more if you prefer, to answer a question. Signal the time with a horn or whistle. If the first pair cannot answer, the next pair can try or choose a different square. If the question remains unanswered, the next pair can try to answer it. If the question is unanswered after all teams have tried, it is out of the game. Tell the children the answer.

4 Time each round. A round should last ten minutes.

5 Play two rounds and add up the scores.

VARIATION 1

Place two or three 'doubles' among your cards. If the children answer correctly they get double the number of the question.

VARIATION 2

Include some fun forfeits among the questions, for example, *Walk like an old man* or *Spell your name backwards*. If they do it, they get the points.

COMMENTS

The success of this game depends on the suitability of the questions. As a rule, the younger the children, the more concrete and curriculum-related the questions should be. Take time throughout the course or year to add to a question file. It will be useful for other activities as well.

Acknowledgements
This game was inspired by the popular US game show *Jeopardy*.

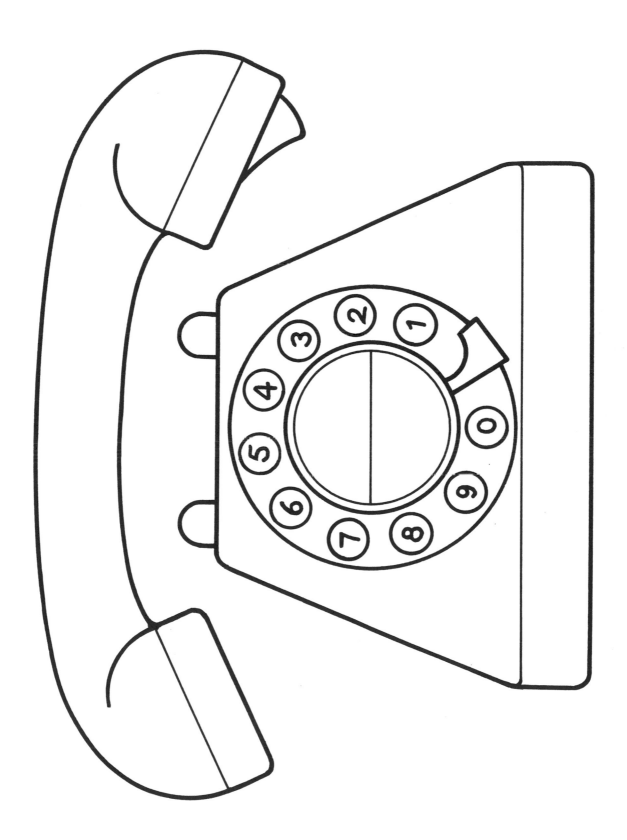

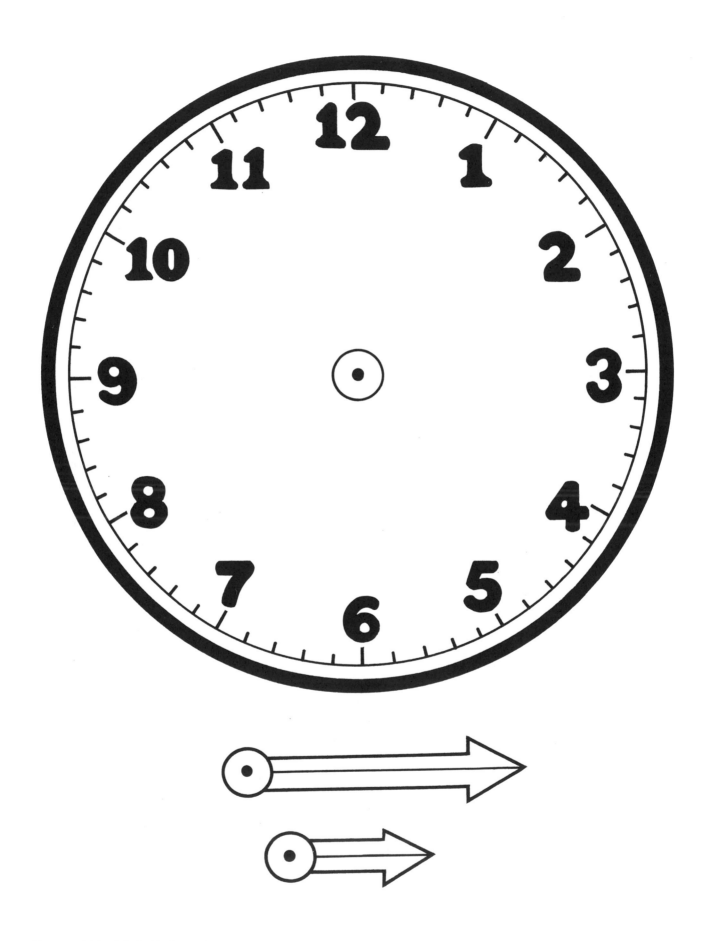

CAGE

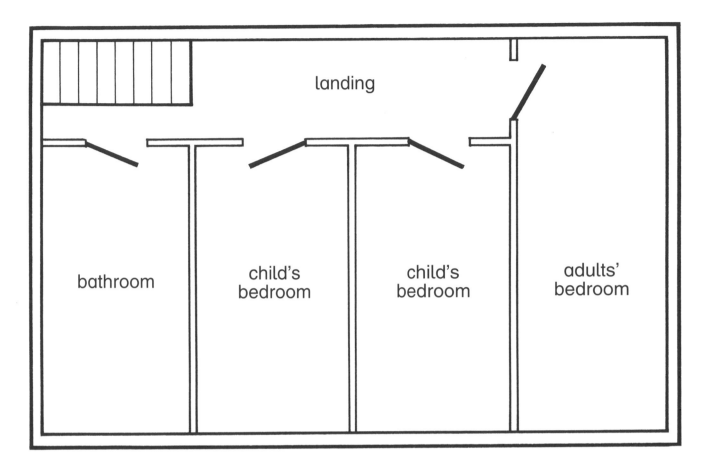

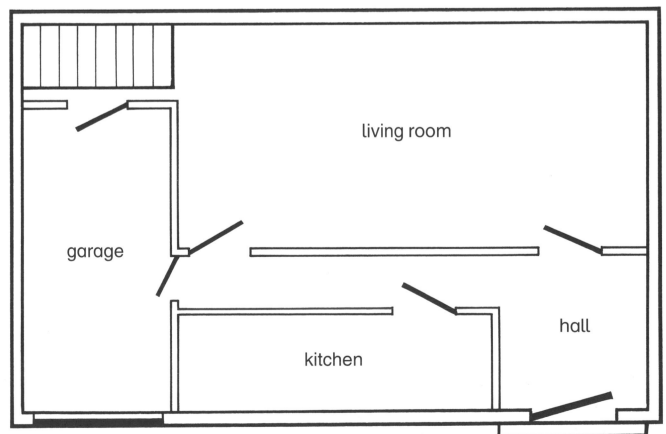

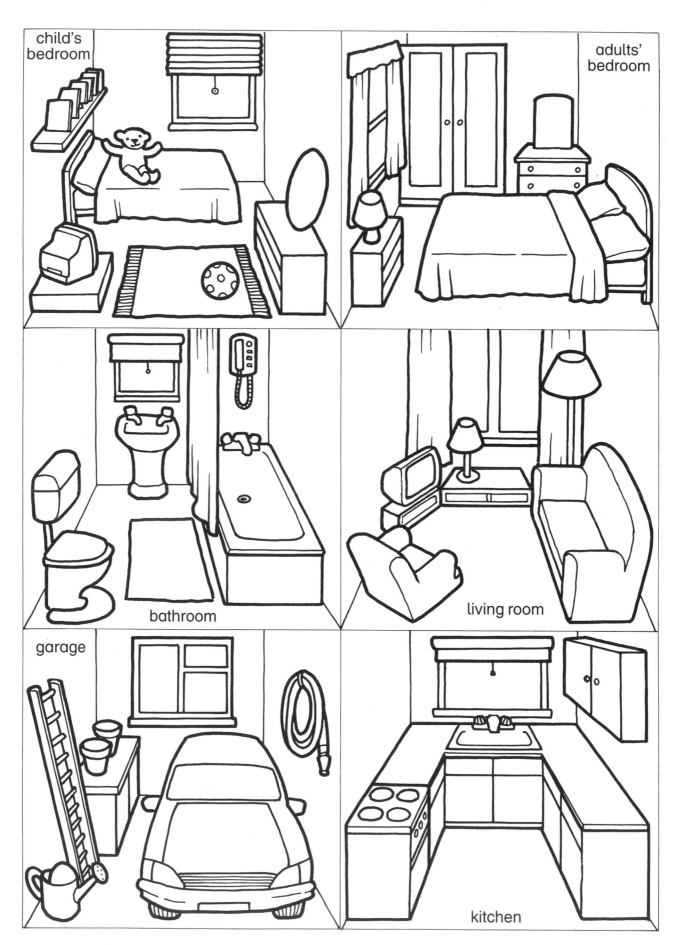

child's bedroom

adults' bedroom

bathroom

living room

garage

kitchen

cow

sheep

chicken

dog

cat

pig

horse

duck

lion

tiger

elephant

zebra

giraffe

parrot

bear

snake

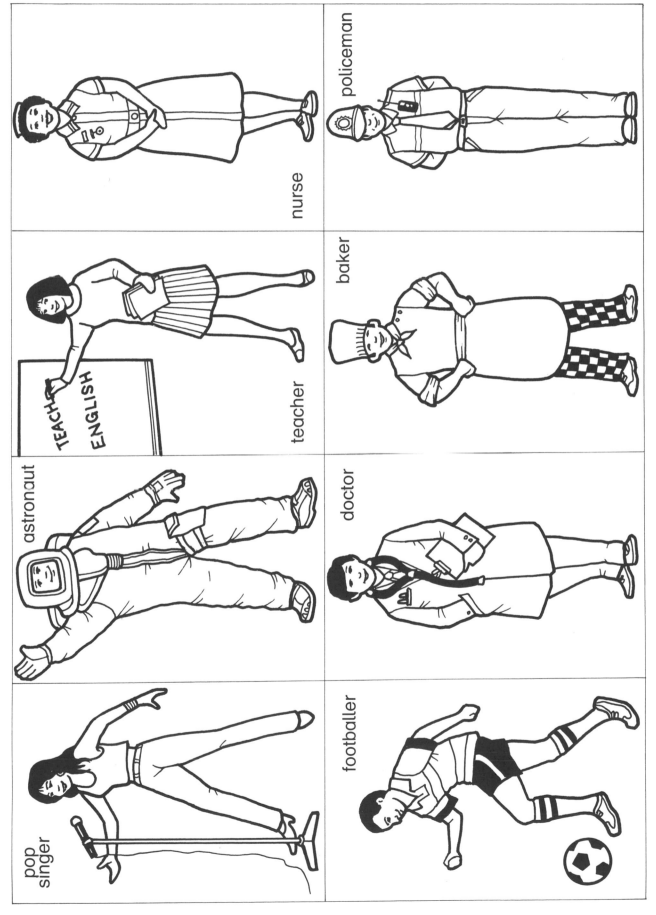

nurse

policeman

teacher

baker

astronaut

doctor

pop singer

footballer

TEACH ENGLISH

Further reading

Background

Brewster, J. 1991. *The Primary English Teacher's Guide*. London: Penguin.

Brown, R. and **D. Monaghan.** 1994. *Teaching Language Skills in Context*. Melbourne: Longman.

Halliwell, S. 1992. *Teaching English in the Primary Classroom*. London: Longman.

Krashen, S. 1987. *Principles and Practice in Second Language Acquisition*. New York: Prentice Hall.

Larsen-Freeman, D. 1991. *An Introduction to Second Language Acquisition Research. London: Longman.*

Linse, C. 1983. *The Children's Response*. Englewood Cliffs: Alemany.

Mackenzie, R. 1996. *Setting Limits in the Classroom*. Rocklin, Ca: Prima.

Matthews, A. and **Read, R.** 1991. *Tandem Plus*. Walton-on-Thames: Nelson.

Collections of games

Cassidy, J. 1993. *Stop the Watch*. Palo Alto: Klutz.

Greenwood, J. 1997. *Activity Box*. Cambridge: Cambridge University Press.

Jackson, S. 1991. *The Book of Classic Board Games*. Palo Alto: Klutz.

Howard-Williams, D. 1994. *Word Games with English*. Oxford: Heinemann.

Kaye, P. 1991. *Games for Learning*. New York: Noonday.

Lee, W. R. 1989. *Language Teaching Games and Contests (2nd edn.)*. Oxford: Oxford University Press.

Palim, J. and **Powers, P.** 1990. *Jamboree*. London: Longman.

Palim, J. and **Powers, P.** 1992. *Tombola*. London: Longman.

Retter, C. and **Valls, N.** 1984. *Bonanza: 77 English Language Games for Young Learners*. London: Longman.

Toth, M. 1995. *Children's Games*. Oxford: Heinemann.

Wingate, J. 1987. *Fun with Faces*. Canterbury: Pilgrims.

Other titles in the Resource Books for Teachers series

Beginners, by Peter Grundy—communicative activities for both absolute and 'false' beginners, including those who do not know the Roman alphabet. All ages. (ISBN 0 19 437200 6)

Class Readers, by Jean Greenwood—activities to develop extensive and intensive reading skills, plus listening and speaking tasks. All ages. (ISBN 0 19 437103 4)

Classroom Dynamics, by Jill Hadfield—helps teachers maintain a good working relationship with their classes, and so promote effective learning. Teenagers and adults. (ISBN 0 19 437147 6)

Conversation, by Rob Nolasco and Lois Arthur—over 80 activities to develop students' ability to speak confidently and fluently. Teenagers and adults. (ISBN 0 19 437096 8)

Creating Stories with Children, by Andrew Wright—encourages creativity, confidence, and fluency and accuracy in spoken and written English. Age 7–14. (ISBN 0 19 437204 9)

Cultural Awareness, by Barry Tomalin and Susan Stempleski—challenges stereotypes, using cultural issues as a rich resource for language practice. Teenagers and adults. (ISBN 0 19 437194 8)

Dictionaries, by Jonathan Wright—ideas for making more effective use of dictionaries in class. Teenagers and adults. (ISBN 019 437219 7)

Drama, by Charlyn Wessels—creative and enjoyable activities using drama to teach spoken communication skills and literature. Teenagers and adults. (ISBN 0 19 437097 6)

Drama with Children, by Sarah Phillips—practical ideas to develop speaking skills, self-confidence, imagination, and creativity. Age 6–12. (ISBN 0 19 437220 0)

Exam Classes, by Peter May—preparation for a wide variety of public examinations, including most of the main American and British exams. Teenagers and adults. (ISBN 0 19 437208 1)

Grammar Dictation, by Ruth Wajnryb—the 'dictogloss' technique—improves understanding and use of grammar by reconstructing texts. Teenagers and adults. (ISBN 0 19 437004 6)

The Internet, by David Eastment, David Hardisty, and Scott Windeatt—motivates learners and brings a wealth of material into the classroom. For all levels of expertise. Teenagers and adults. (ISBN 0 19 437223 5)

Learner-based Teaching, by Colin Campbell and Hanna Kryszewska—unlocks the wealth of knowledge that learners bring to the classroom. All ages. (ISBN 0 19 437163 8)

Letters, by Nicky Burbidge, Peta Gray, Sheila Levy, and Mario Rinvolucri—using letters and e-mail for language and cultural study. Teenagers and adults. (ISBN 0 19 442149 X)

Listening, by Goodith White—advice and ideas for encouraging learners to become 'active listeners'. Teenagers and adults. (ISBN 0 19 437216 2)

Literature, by Alan Maley and Alan Duff—an innovatory book on using literature for language practice. Teenagers and adults. (ISBN 0 19 437094 1)

Music and Song, by Tim Murphey—'tuning in' to students' musical tastes can increase motivation and tap a rich vein of resources. All ages. (ISBN 0 19 437055 0)

Newspapers, by Peter Grundy—original ideas for making effective use of newspapers in lessons. Teenagers and adults. (ISBN 0 19 437192 6)

Projects with Young Learners, by Diane Phillips, Sarah Burwood, and Helen Dunford—encourages learner independence by producing a real sense of achievement. Age 5 to 13. (ISBN 0 19 437221 9)

Project Work, by Diana L. Fried-Booth—bridges the gap between the classroom and the outside world. Teenagers and adults. (ISBN 0 19 437092 5)

Pronunciation, by Clement Laroy—imaginative activities to build confidence and improve all aspects of pronunciation. All ages. (ISBN 0 19 437087 9)

Role Play, by Gillian Porter Ladousse—controlled conversations to improvised drama, simple dialogues to complex scenarios. Teenagers and adults. (ISBN 0 19 437095 X)

Self-Access, by Susan Sheerin—advice on setting up and managing self-access study facilities, plus materials. Teenagers and adults. (ISBN 0 19 437099 2)

Storytelling with Children, by Andrew Wright—hundreds of exciting ideas for using stories to teach English to children aged 7 to 14. (ISBN 0 19 437202 2)

Translation, by Alan Duff—a wide variety of translation activities from many different subject areas. Teenagers and adults. (ISBN 0 19 437104 2)

Very Young Learners, by Vanessa Reilly and Sheila M. Ward—advice and ideas for teaching children aged 3 to 6 years, including games, songs, drama, stories, and art and crafts. (ISBN 0 19 437209 X)

Video, by Richard Cooper, Mike Lavery, and Mario Rinvolucri—original ideas for watching and making videos. All ages. (ISBN 0 19 437102 6)

Vocabulary, by John Morgan and Mario Rinvolucri—a wide variety of communicative activities for teaching new words. Teenagers and adults. (ISBN 437091 7)

Writing, by Tricia Hedge—a wide range of writing tasks, as well as guidance on student difficulties with writing. Teenagers and adults. (ISBN 0 19 437098 4)

Young Learners, by Sarah Phillips—advice and ideas for teaching English to children aged 6–12, including arts and crafts, games, stories, poems, and songs. (ISBN 0 19 437195 6)

Index of game types

Often it is convenient to look for a game by type when planning a lesson. Here we have grouped the games according to their outstanding feature. Please note, however, that many games are hybrids and may contain components of other game types as well.

Index of language

You may find it helpful to search for games by their most prominent language focus or function. Please note that there are many other possible language focuses and functions in the variations. For vocabulary on particular topics, see the chapter headings.

Index of non-linguistic skills

OXFORD
UNIVERSITY PRESS

English Language Teaching Division

Dear Teacher

We would like your views on how best to develop the *Resource Books for Teachers* series. We would be very grateful if you could fill in this questionnaire and return it to the address at the bottom. We are offering a free OUP wallchart to everyone who returns this form, and a free Resource Book each for the ten most informative replies received every month.

About yourself

Your name _____

Address _____

_____

_____

Are you: ☐ A teacher?   ☐ A teacher trainer?   ☐ A trainee teacher?

Other? (Please specify) _____

What type of establishment do you work in?

_____

What age are your students?   ☐ 3–6   ☐ 6–12   ☐ 12–17   ☐ 18+

How many students per class?   ☐ under 15   ☐ 15–30   ☐ over 30

Which teachers' resource book(s) do you use most (from any publisher)?

_____

Which topic(s) would you most like to see in a new Resource Book for Teachers?

_____

_____

About
Games for Children

What do you find most useful about this book?

☐ New ideas for class   ☐ Advice in the Introduction

☐ Other _____

Is there anything you **don't** like about the book?

_____

_____

For teachers in your situation:

Is the amount of knowledge assumed   ☐ too high   ☐ just right   ☐ too low?

Is the language in the book   ☐ easy to read   ☐ too difficult?

What do you think of the cover design?

_____

Do you photocopy the worksheets?   Yes/No

Do you adapt the activities for your classes?   Yes/No

Do you make your own materials?   Yes/No

Any other comments? *(You can continue your comments on a separate sheet if you wish.)*

_____

_____

Please send your reply to:

Julia Sallabank
Senior Editor, ELT
Oxford University Press
Great Clarendon Street
Oxford
OX2 6DP
UK

Thank you very much for taking the time to answer this questionnaire.

Which wallchart would you prefer?

☐ Map of the UK and world   ☐ Birthday song (primary)

☐ Map of the USA   ☐ Town scene with worksheets (primary)

☐ English sounds (IPA symbols)

Which Resource Book for Teachers would you prefer? (See the list on pages 146–7.)